DO YOU KNOW...

Who was Genghis Khan?

    a) a character in a *Star Trek* movie

    b) the bloodthirsty ruler of the Mongol Empire

    c) the founder of a hot dog and cold cuts empire

What is a "Bun Pup"?

    a) a strange-looking dog

    b) a vegetarian who eats only bread

    c) waiters' slang for a hot dog

Who were Athos, Porthos, and Aramis?

    a) the Three Musketeers

    b) statesmen who met at the Yalta Conference in 1945
       during World War II

    c) famous designers with their own signature fragrances

**FIND OUT THE ANSWERS
TO THESE QUESTIONS...
AND MANY MORE QUESTIONS
YOU DIDN'T EVEN KNOW YOU HAD!**

KID STUFF

People, Places, and
Things to Know

BY MARGO McLOONE BASTA
AND ALICE SIEGEL

A BANTAM SKYLARK BOOK
New York • Toronto • London • Sydney • Auckland

RL 4, 007–012

KID STUFF

A Bantam Skylark Book / November 1991

*Skylark Books is a registered trademark of Bantam Books,
a division of Bantam Doubleday Dell Publishing Group, Inc.
Registered in U.S. Patent and Trademark Office and elsewhere.*

ISBN 0-553-15914-3

Published simultaneously in the United States and Canada

*Bantam Books are published by Bantam Books, a division of Bantam
Doubleday Dell Publishing Group, Inc. Its trademark, consisting of the
words ''Bantam Books'' and the portrayal of a rooster, is Registered
in U.S. Patent and Trademark Office and in other countries. Marca
Registrada. Bantam Books, 666 Fifth Avenue, New York, New York
10103.*

Printed in the United States of America

OPM *0 9 8 7 6 5 4 3 2 1*

For my son William, who was born
with this book.
—M.M.B.

For my wonderful husband George, sons
Andrew, Howard, and James—who will
forever be my most severe critics.
—A.S.

Thanks to my husband, Douglas, and my daughters, Catherine and Elizabeth, who challenge and inspire me.
Special thanks to three Woodstock librarians: Judy Fischetti, Jane Letus, and Joann Sackett. They have been generous and cheerful with their time and help.
—M.M.B.

Special thanks to the folks behind the reference desk at the Greenwich Public Library and the dedicated teaching staff at Hamilton Avenue School, Greenwich, Connecticut.
—A.S.

──────────────

• • • • • • • • • • • • • •

CONTENTS

· ·

INTRODUCTION

. . . .

You've probably heard of "good stuff"; it's what a baseball pitcher has when he's throwing lively pitches. You've probably heard of "the right stuff"; it's the special trait needed to become a fighter pilot. In this book you can find "kid stuff"—some of the things you need to know in order to be informed about the world you live in. With *Kid Stuff: People, Places, and Things to Know* you can better understand what you read in newspapers, books, and magazines, and what you hear in movies, songs, and conversations. You'll find information about people from our literature and history, places both real and imaginary, and facts from our culture, such as the lingo that's used to order food in diners. *Kid Stuff: People, Places, and Things to Know* can be used as a reference book, or just for fun reading. Either way, it's got the stuff smart kids want to know about!

. . . .

KID STUFF

SECTION I:

PEOPLE TO KNOW

How can you know and remember all the people who have made their mark in history? In the section that follows some of the most famous people in the world are grouped into categories that are easy to remember. Included are adventurers and wanderers who set out to explore the world, and nasty villains who wanted to take over the world. There are lovers who gave up their lives for each other, outlaws known for their terrible greed, and rivals and foes who battled to their deaths.

. . . .

ADVENTURERS

• •

Adventurers are people who leave behind a familiar world to explore an unknown one. Adventurers such as Neil Armstrong and Beryl Markham risked their lives entering a new territory. The discoveries made by adventurers trying new feats often benefit all of humanity.

Neil Armstrong (1930–   )

Neil Armstrong, an American astronaut, was the first human to set foot on Earth's moon. Armstrong was the mission commander and only civilian member of the *Apollo 11* crew, which also included Air Force officers Edwin (Buzz) Aldrin and Michael Collins.

Apollo 11 traveled 244,930 miles over four days. As planned, the lunar landing module *Eagle* separated from the *Apollo 11* on July 20, 1969, and began its descent to the moon. However, Armstrong, who was aboard the *Eagle* with Aldrin, quickly noticed that the preselected command module landing site was covered with large rocks. He switched over to manual control and guided the *Eagle* to a safe landing on a smooth surface. When Armstrong stepped out of the module and set foot on the moon, he said, "That's one small step for a man, one giant leap for mankind." After twenty-one-and-a-half hours on the moon, the *Eagle* lifted off, docked with the mother ship, and returned to Earth.

Nellie Bly (1867–1922)

Nellie Bly was the pen name of a nineteenth-century American journalist, whose real name was Elizabeth Cochrane. In 1889, she took up the challenge of Phileas Fogg, the character in Jules Verne's novel *Around the World in Eighty Days*, who bets he can circle the globe within eighty days. Nellie Bly's trip around the world was financed by her newspaper, *The World*, and she set sail from New York in 1889. Traveling by ship, train, ricksha (a two-wheeled vehicle pulled by one or two men), and burro, the reporter returned home in just seventy-two days. She wrote her story, *Around the World in Seventy-two Days*, in 1890.

Christopher Columbus (1451–1506)

Christopher Columbus's exploits were a turning point in the history of travel. For many years he was thought to be the first European to discover the Americas. Columbus was born in humble surroundings in Italy in the fifteenth century. As a boy he was fascinated by sea travel and Marco Polo's writings about his travels to the Orient. When he reached manhood, he petitioned the courts of Europe to supply him with a fleet so that he might sail west to the Orient, something never before attempted. Finally, in 1492, with three ships provided by the Spanish court, he set sail. He had to keep morale high among his crew, who were frightened to be so far from shore in unknown waters. Columbus calmed them by promising to turn back if no land was sighted within three days. The crew sighted an island in the Caribbean Sea, just in time. Although he was lost trying to find a new way to the Orient, he found land, now known as the Americas.

Columbus was a great navigator. He had exceptional eyesight and a keen sense of smell and direction. The outward and homeward bound routes he chose are still used today for transatlantic sea travel.

In his lifetime Columbus made four voyages to America but failed to reach the Orient. When he died at the age of fifty-five, he was bitterly disappointed and had been disgraced by the envy of his rivals. It took time and the lessons of history to establish him as an important figure in world discovery.

James Cook (1728–1779)

Captain James Cook was an English adventurer, explorer, and scientist. He covered more sea distance, discovered more new land, and added more to human knowledge of the earth than any other person of his time.

On three separate voyages in the late eighteenth century, he sailed to Tahiti, was the first European to sail to New Zealand, Australia, and Hawaii, explored Antarctica, and traveled to Alaska. Everywhere he went he examined plant life, animals, and the geography of the land and sea. He fought outbreaks of scurvy aboard his ship by a method unusual for the times—carrying vegetables and fruit along with the usual salt pork and hardtack. Captain Cook died on the island of Hawaii, after a scuffle with the natives.

Amelia Earhart (1898–1937)

Amelia Earhart disappeared over the Pacific Ocean in 1937 when she attempted to fly around the world.

Even as a child Amelia was daring. She built her own roller coaster, and fearlessly rode down snow-covered hills in the fastest sled. At the age of twenty-two, she learned how to fly. When she got her pilot's license, she was one of about a dozen women pilots in the world. In 1928 she was the first female passenger on a transatlantic flight. But Amelia Earhart wanted to pilot, not simply ride along with someone else at the controls. Four years later she flew alone across the Atlantic from Newfoundland to Ireland. After that she became the first woman to fly alone across the U.S. in both directions. She set many long-distance flying records, but her ultimate goal was to fly around the world. On March 17, 1937 she started out from California in her plane, the *Flying Laboratory*, heading west. Her plane developed problems in Hawaii, however, and was brought back to California for repairs. She then set off from Florida and traveled as far as

New Guinea. Somewhere over the Pacific, near Howland Island, she was lost forever. In early 1991 debris was found on a remote South Pacific island. Investigators speculated that the debris was from Earhart's plane.

Hannibal (247–183 B.C.)

Hannibal was a statesman and general of the ancient city of Carthage in North Africa. He lived in the second century B.C., and was raised by a father who instilled in him an intense dislike of Rome. During the Second Punic War between Rome and Carthage, Hannibal was a commander of forces in Spain. Setting out for Rome with his huge army, he crossed the Pyrenees Mountains into France, then headed over the Alps into Italy. He and his men then traveled on the backs of elephants across the Rhône River. When Hannibal finally arrived in Rome, he had lost many men to the cold and fighting. Because he was unable to overcome Rome, he returned to Carthage. The Romans came after him there. Rather than surrender to his hated foe, he committed suicide. Hannibal's leading of his troops across the Alps is considered one of the greatest adventures and military feats of all time.

David Livingstone (1813–1873)

Dr. David Livingstone, a Scottish explorer and missionary, went in 1841 to explore Africa and serve the medical needs of the African natives. When Livingstone witnessed the evil ways of the slave traders, he and his family moved far into the interior to escape them.

In Livingstone's lifetime he traveled over 29,000 miles, charting the African jungles on foot. When the world believed that Livingstone had been lost, a young American reporter, Henry Stanley, went in search of him. After looking for eleven months, Stanley found Livingstone working with a local African tribe. Stanley greeted him with words that have since become famous, "Doctor Livingstone, I presume?" At the age of sixty, Livingstone died of jungle fever. His beloved Africans buried his heart where he died, deep in the African jungle. His embalmed body was then carried a thousand miles across the continent to a ship that was waiting to carry him to England. Dr. Livingstone is buried in Westminster Abbey with other notable Englishmen.

Beryl Markham (1902–1986)

Beryl Markham was a well-known aviator. She was born in England, then moved with her father to Kenya, Africa, when she was four. As a youngster she tracked and hunted wild animals in the bush with native Muranai tribesmen. She survived being mauled by a neighbor's "pet" lion. As a young woman she became Africa's first female horse trainer. Later she became Africa's first female professional pilot. She worked as a bush pilot scouting elephant herds for safari hunters. Her greatest feat was to be the first person to fly solo across the Atlantic from England to America. She survived the twenty-one-hour flight and crash-landed in Nova Scotia, Canada. Beryl Markham wrote the story of her remarkable life in her memoirs, *West with the Night*.

Marco Polo (1254–1324?)

Marco Polo's adventures in the Orient opened the minds of Europeans who knew little or nothing of the world of Asia. Marco was raised in Venice, Italy, in the thirteenth century. He saw little of his father, who spent most of his time traveling in China. When Marco was a young man his father returned to Italy with fascinating stories of the Orient. At the age of seventeen, Marco went to China with his father. They spent time at the court of Kublai Khan, the Mongol emperor. The Khan asked Marco to explore his vast kingdom and report back to him about the people and sights he had seen. For twenty-four years Marco toured South China, Burma, Indochina, and Indonesia. He went to Siberia. He journeyed across the Gobi Desert. He rode camels and horses and sailed on ships. He learned four languages, all of which he spoke fluently. After traveling 15,000 miles, he returned to Italy and wrote his memoirs in a book he called *Description of the World*. (The title he ended up with is *The Travels of Marco Polo*.) The book fascinated Europeans with its descriptions of the wonders of the Orient. Marco Polo ranks as one of the great travelers and adventurers of all time.

Sacagawea (1784–1884)

Sacagawea (Bird Woman) was a Shoshone Indian of Idaho. When she was a young girl she was captured by an enemy tribe and taken to North Dakota, where she married a French-Canadian trader, Touissant Charbonneau. When Lewis and Clark made their famous expedition to the Northeast Territory, they enlisted sixteen-year-old Sacagawea's help as a guide. She led them across the Rocky Mountains to the Pacific Ocean. She carried her newborn baby, Jean-Baptiste (whose Shoshone name was Sun Pomp), on her back for the entire trip. She helped the party survive by gathering wild foods and making pemmican (cured buffalo meat), and she obtained horses from Indian tribes. She acted as an emissary to tribes who might have otherwise seen the expedition party as hostile. Sacagawea was an invaluable help to the Lewis and Clark expedition.

WANDERERS

•••••••••••••••••••••••••••••••••••••••

Wanderers are people who roam about without a specific destination. Some wanderers, such as Johnny Appleseed, left visible reminders behind when they traveled. Others, such as Sojourner Truth, left less obvious reminders, but are memorable still.

Real Wanderers

Hans Christian Andersen (1805–1875)

Hans Christian Andersen was born in Denmark in 1805. As a young man he failed as an actor and began wandering the countryside telling stories to village children. Later he visited many European cities, telling his tales. Andersen wrote a total of 168 fairy tales, including "The Emperor's New Clothes" and "The Ugly Duckling." This wandering storyteller became one of Denmark's greatest authors and a world-renowned storyteller.

Johnny Appleseed (1774–1845)

John Chapman, better known as Johnny Appleseed, was born in Massachusetts on September 26, 1774. He was a professional nurseryman who became a legend when he wandered from the East Coast to the Midwest, planting apple seeds along the way. Stories about him spread. It was said he wore an eccentric outfit, which included three layers of hats. The first hat had a wide brim; the second was his cooking pot; and the third was a crown. On one foot he wore an old shoe tied on with strings; on the other foot was an old boot. When Johnny Appleseed wasn't planting seeds, he was often seen standing around eating apples. In the course of his travels, he often returned to prune the orchards he created. Today the apple trees he planted still grow by some roadsides.

Sojourner Truth (1797–1883)

Sojourner Truth was born a slave in 1797. Her name was Isabella Baumfree. She was freed in 1827. In 1843, she took a new name, Sojourner Truth, which means a traveler who spreads truth. For more than forty years she traveled across the U.S., speaking out against slavery and for women's rights. She often said, "To be good in the eyes of God, you must do good to all his children." During her travels she met other famous abolitionists, among them, ex-slave Frederick Douglass; the author of *Uncle Tom's Cabin*, Harriet Beecher Stowe; and President Abraham Lincoln.

Fictional Wanderers

Don Quixote

Don Quixote (Don kee-HO-tay) is a fictitious character who wanders around the Spanish countryside hoping to right a corrupt world. He is the comical hero of Don Miguel de Cervantes's seventeenth-century novel, *Don Quixote*. Though dressed in rusty armor, Quixote fancies himself a knight in shining armor. His companion in his travels is his "squire," Sancho Panza. Everywhere Quixote and Panza go, they find commonplace objects to be fearsome. Most famous is Quixote's battle with windmills, which he mistakes for giants.

• • • • • • • • • • • •

Odysseus

Odysseus is a mythical Greek hero. After fighting for Greece against Troy, he begins a long journey home. For ten years he wanders, visiting the land of the lotus eaters, where magic food makes travelers forget their home; fighting the Cyclops, a one-eyed monster who imprisons him; and surviving many hardships and challenges. *The Odyssey*, written by Homer, is a long poem that tells of Odysseus' wanderings. The name Odysseus is now synonymous with wanderer, and an odyssey is a journey.

Peer Gynt

Peer Gynt is the main character in Henrik Ibsen's dramatic poem of the same name. Ibsen based his hero on a real person who lived in Norway at the end of the nineteenth century. Ibsen is said to have used him as the basis for a "Nordic Everyman." Ibsen's Peer Gynt is a wanderer who spends his life bouncing from place to place and rushing headlong into trouble. Some of his adventures include the kidnapping of a neighbor's daughter on her wedding day, and involvement with a troll, which leads to his fathering a monster. At the end of his life and fifty years of wandering, Peer realizes he is wiser about the world and himself.

Pied Piper

The Pied Piper was a legendary figure of thirteenth-century Europe. According to the story, he was a musician who wandered into a rat-infested village, Hamelin, Germany. There he was hired to rid the town of rats. He did so by playing his silver pipe and leading the rats away. When the town refused to pay him for his service, he led the children of Hamelin away in the same manner. Neither the Pied Piper nor the children were ever seen in the village again.

INFAMOUS PEOPLE

Our history is filled with infamous people, people who have become famous because of their evil deeds. Sometimes the bad guys or gals can be almost likable, or perceived as glamorous, as in the case of Bonnie and Clyde. But most of the time, especially when the infamous characters are real people, such as Adolf Hitler, who have committed terrible crimes, they are remembered with horror.

Murderers

Lizzie Borden (1860–1927)

> **Lizzie Borden took an ax,**
> **And gave her mother forty whacks;**
> **And when she saw what she had done**
> **She gave her father forty-one.**

This is the famous rhyme about Lizzie Borden, a woman who was accused, but never convicted, of the murder of her father and stepmother. In 1892, at the age of thirty-two, Lizzie Borden was living at home with her parents in Falls River, Massachusetts. One day her parents were found hacked to death by an ax. Lizzie and Bridget Sullivan, a housemaid, were the only other people living in the house at the time. The ax was found in the basement. Lizzie was accused of the murder by her brother and sister and the police. It was said she hated her stepmother and barely spoke to her father. She was tried for the murder but was found innocent. Lizzie Borden inherited a great deal of money and lived out the rest of her life as a recluse.

Jack the Ripper (dates unknown)

In 1888 a man called Jack the Ripper terrorized the women of London, England. He brutally murdered and mutilated five women. Although he taunted the police, he continually evaded them. On November 9, 1888, he committed his last known murder and completely vanished. His identity was never known. Jack the Ripper is one of the most infamous mass murderers of all times.

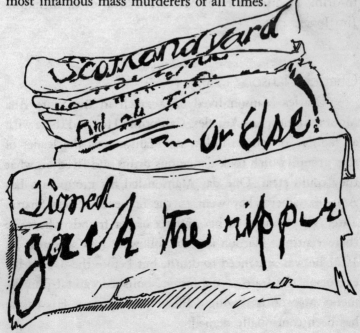

Jim Jones (1931–1978)

Jim Jones was an ordained minister who convinced hundreds of people to follow him. In order to belong to his ministry, people were asked to give up their families, jobs, and homes to live communally at Jones's Peoples Temple. By 1972 Jones claimed to have raised forty people from the dead. He also declared himself to be a reincarnation of Jesus Christ and Buddha. He was having visions and describing his powers as godlike. Finally, he declared himself God, and his followers were ordered to worship him. He moved to Guyana, South America, and built a city called Jonestown. He brought eight hundred followers with him. In 1978 he led his followers to their deaths by asking them to drink a poisoned Kool-Aid. Almost all died, including Jim Jones.

Charles Manson (1934–   )

Charles Manson lived on a ranch in the Santa Ana Mountains near Los Angeles, California. He lived there with a "family" of female followers. Manson was the leader of this group, which took dangerous drugs and lived on what they could steal. One day Manson led his group into Los Angeles, where they went to the home of actress Sharon Tate. They murdered her and six of her friends who were there visiting. Manson and his followers were arrested. In 1971 he was sentenced to death, but before the date of his execution the state of California abolished capital punishment. Manson is serving a life term in prison. His parole has been continually denied.

Outlaws

Ma Barker (1872–1935)

Kate Barker raised four sons, Herman, Lloyd, Arthur, and Fred, whom she trained to commit robberies, kidnappings, and murders. By 1922 the Barkers had made off with three million dollars in stolen money. Then the law caught up with them. Herman was shot; Lloyd was sentenced to twenty-five years in jail; Arthur and Fred were sentenced to jail but soon released. After that Ma Barker planned a kidnapping of two wealthy businessmen and used Arthur and Fred to pull it off. In 1935 the FBI tracked the three of them down. Arthur was captured and Fred and Ma died in a shootout. It remains a mystery whether Ma Barker was shot by the FBI agents or whether she shot herself to avoid being captured.

Billy the Kid (1859–1881)

William Bonney was born in New York, but moved to New Mexico with his mother and brother after the death of his father. Billy was only fourteen when his mother died, leaving him alone and adrift in the Wild West. As some stories go, Billy became an outlaw when he was fifteen years old. A man insulted Billy, and Billy killed him. From then on he lived the life of a fugitive, running, fighting, and killing. He once claimed to have killed twenty-one people: "One for every year of my life." In 1881 Billy was caught and killed by Sheriff Pat Garrett. Garrett said of Billy the Kid, "Those who knew him best will tell you that in his most savage and dangerous mood his face always wore a smile."

Bonnie and Clyde (1910–1934) (1909–1934)

Bonnie Parker met Clyde Barrow in Dallas, Texas, in the early 1930s. She was working as a waitress in a café and her husband was in jail serving a life sentence. She teamed up with Clyde, a drifter, and the two set out across Texas and the Southwest. They were small-time thieves who stole from gas stations, cafés, and banks. They murdered ruthlessly, once shooting a man for ten dollars. They enjoyed publicity and public notoriety, often sending pictures of themselves in their hideouts to the newspapers. Bonnie called herself "Suicide Sal" and Clyde was named "Public Enemy #1 of the Southwest." In 1934 a friend told the authorities where the two could be found. The Texas Rangers ambushed them on a highway, and they were both killed in the shootout.

John Dillinger (1903–1934)

In the early 1920s, the FBI named John Dillinger Public Enemy #1. He was a notorious bank robber who daringly raided police stations for weapons. His career as an outlaw began at the age of nineteen when he robbed a grocery store. The robbery was unsuccessful. He was arrested and sent to prison. After his release, he went on to rob and kill throughout the North Central states, becoming responsible for sixteen murders. When the FBI began searching for him he went into hiding. He dyed his hair, had his face lifted, and used an acid treatment to alter his fingerprints. In 1934 an acquaintance told the FBI where he could be found. He was shot down outside a movie theater in Chicago.

John Wesley Hardin (1853–1895)

In the violent history of the American West, John Wesley Hardin is known as the worst murderer of all. He killed a man for the first time at the age of fifteen, and went on to kill well over twenty men. For one of his many murders he served fifteen years in jail. A few years after he was released he set up a law office in El Paso, Texas. During this time he spent much of his time in saloons, gambling. In 1895 Hardin was shot to death in a saloon.

Jesse James (1847–1882)

Jesse James and his brother, Frank, were guerilla fighters against the Union in the Civil War. So were Cole Younger and his brother Jim. After the war, they were branded outlaws and hunted by Union soldiers. After being joined by the other two Younger brothers, Robert and John, they formed a gang that was soon famous for their daring bank and train robberies throughout the Midwest. They were often hidden and protected by relatives or Confederate sympathizers. Their robbing and killing spree almost ended in an attempted bank robbery in Northfield, Minnesota, when some members of the gang were killed and others were captured. Frank and Jesse James escaped. The reward for Jesse's capture was so great he was finally shot in his own home by one of his new gang members in 1882. Despite his wrongdoings, Jesse was considered a hero by many Americans. Ballads have been written about him and more than twenty movies have been made about his life.

Real Pirates

Blackbeard (1680?–1718)

Captain Edward Teach called himself Blackbeard. He had a long black beard, which was often braided and tied with colored ribbons. During battle he would frighten his enemies by lighting cannon fuses in his beard and surrounding his head with smoke. He dressed completely in black and wore many knives and pistols. He sailed the Caribbean Sea, ruthlessly preying on other ships. He was known to cut off the finger of any man who wouldn't give up his ring to him. He married fourteen women and left them all. Finally the crew members of a British ship caught him and killed him. It took five bullets and twenty deep slashes to do him in. His head was later dangled from a ship's prow and paraded through the ports of North Carolina as a warning to other pirates.

William Kidd (c. 1645–1701)

In 1695 Captain Kidd was hired as a privateer to stop piracy against English ships. While he was supposed to be looking for pirates in the Indian Ocean, he became a pirate. There are stories of his cruelty and of treasures he buried along the eastern coast of the U.S. No one knows if these stories are true. What is known is that he was captured by the British, found guilty of piracy, then shot to death and hanged.

Read and Bonney (1680–1720/1) (1700–?)

Mary Read and Anne Bonney are the most famous women pirates in history. They served together on the same pirate ship, both disguised as men. It is said that on board, they learned of each other's hidden identities and became good friends. When their pirate ship was attacked in 1720 they were the only two to remain on deck to fight. In the end, the entire crew was captured. Both women were sentenced to hang for piracy. While waiting for their sentences, Mary Read died of fever in her prison cell. Anne Bonney was allowed to go free. No one knows what happened to her.

Fictional Pirates

Captain Hook

Perhaps the most famous fictional pirate is Captain Hook from the play *Peter Pan* by J. M. Barrie. Captain Hook is the fearsome captain of the pirate ship the *Jolly Roger*, who wears an iron claw on his right arm after a duel in which Peter Pan cut off Hook's right hand and threw it to a crocodile. Hook then roams Never-Never Land hunting for Peter Pan and the Lost Boys. The pirate meets his end in another duel with Peter Pan, when Peter is trying to rescue Wendy, John, and Michael Darling and the Lost Boys from Hook's ship. In this final fight, Peter kicks Hook overboard, into the jaws of the same crocodile who had eaten his hand.

Long John Silver

In the novel *Treasure Island*, by Robert Louis Stevenson, Long John Silver is the murderous pirate with one leg. He uses his easy-going manner to bargain and charm his way to Treasure Island. Throughout the story he changes his loyalties to suit himself. In the end he is captured and taken back to England to stand trial for piracy. However, he manages to slip away with some of the treasure and is never seen or heard from again.

Villainous Rulers

Idi Amin (1925–   )

Idi Amin, the one-time president of Uganda, has been called the mass murderer of the 1970s. In 1971 he seized control of his African country and began to expel the entire Asian population. He then began to purge the native tribes of his enemies. He was responsible for the deaths of more than 90,000 people before he was driven into exile in 1979.

Attila the Hun (406–453)

Attila, king of the Huns, ruled his nomadic people of north central Asia early in the fifth century. He was a short man with a broad chest, swarthy complexion, and pinlike eyes. He could neither read nor write, but he could fight. He led his tribesmen in the conquest and destruction of land from Mongolia to Italy. Because of his savagery, Attila was known as the "scourge of God." He massacred entire villages in his conquest. Attila died suddenly at the age of forty-seven when blood from his nose pooled in his throat one night and suffocated him.

Bloody Mary (1516–1558)

Mary Tudor was the first woman to rule England in her own right. She was the daughter of King Henry VIII and his first wife, Catherine of Aragon. When her father divorced her mother, he became a Protestant. Most of the country changed from Catholic to Protestant at that time.

Those that did not convert were persecuted, killed, or driven out of the country. Some remained, including Mary, who secretly stayed Catholic. In 1553 she succeeded her Protestant brother to the throne. She wanted to bring Catholicism back to England, so she began to persecute the Protestants. She earned the name "Bloody Mary" by having more than three hundred Protestants burned at the stake.

Caligula (12–41)

Caligula became the emperor of the Roman Empire at the age of twenty-five. A true egomaniac, he declared, "I have the right to do anything to anybody." He was tall, fat-bellied, and hollow-eyed, with a large bald spot on his head. He was so jealous of men with full heads of hair, he would often order their heads shaved to show large bald spots like his own. During his four-year term he committed hideous crimes against his subjects. He shut down public granaries so people would starve and tortured his enemies by inflicting them with numerous slight wounds, until they died an agonizingly slow death. He killed people just to use their blood in plays performed for him. When he was assassinated in A.D. 41, at the age of twenty-nine, the people of Rome celebrated his death.

Nicolae Ceausescu (1918–1989)

Nicolae Ceausescu came to power in Romania in 1965. He was an iron-handed dictator who lived in excessive luxury while he rationed fuel and food to the people of Romania.

He had a paranoid personality and always feared his enemies would poison him. He carried his own food with him when he traveled, kept his clothes under lock and key so they wouldn't be poisoned, and wore a different suit each day, then had it burned.

In 1989 Ceausescu was captured and tried for genocide. He was found guilty and executed on Christmas Day. Under his dictatorship more than 64,000 innocent people of Romania were killed. After his government was toppled, Tass, the Soviet news agency, termed him "one of the most odious dictators of the twentieth century."

Henry VIII (1491-1547)

Henry the VIII was a ruthless, heartless king who ruled England from 1509 to 1547. Though his subjects lived in relative peace during his reign, those who were close to him did not. Henry was a Catholic when he married his first wife, Catherine of Aragon. They had one daughter, but Henry wanted a son who would be an heir to his throne. Because divorce was not allowed in the Catholic religion, he became a Protestant and divorced Catherine. He then married Anne Boleyn, grew tired of her, and had her beheaded. His next wife, Jane Seymour, died giving birth to a son. He then married Anne of Cleves and later divorced her. Next he married Catherine Howard and had her beheaded. His sixth and final wife was Catherine Parr.

During his reign Henry also had his good friend Thomas More beheaded because of More's devout Catholic beliefs and objections to divorce. Henry VIII eliminated many Catholics who resisted the country's change to Protestantism.

Adolf Hitler (1889–1945)

Adolf Hitler is remembered as the great villain of the twentieth century. He founded the Nazi party in 1920 and later became dictator of Germany. As a ruler, Hitler controlled all facets of German life. His anti-Semitic beliefs became law and he systematically imprisoned Jews in concentration camps and eliminated six million of them. He waged war against the rest of Europe in his attempt to bring the world under the power of his Third Reich. The result was World War II. His dreadful tyranny ended in 1945, when he was defeated by the Allies and committed suicide.

Genghis Khan (1167?–1227)

When Genghis Khan was nine years old, his father was poisoned by feuding Mongol tribesmen. Genghis Khan grew up determined to avenge his father's death and eliminate all rivals. He succeeded in uniting the tribes into a single Mongol nation, which he ruled alone. His greed for power led him to conquer much of Asia. He and his tribesmen began their bloody invasions in 1206. Most often they massacred entire cities. Sometimes they took prisoners and forced them to march as front soldiers against their own neighbors. Everywhere the troops of Genghis Khan went, they laid waste to the land and destroyed fine, old artifacts of civilization. When Genghis Khan died in 1227, his empire stretched from Eastern Europe to the Sea of Japan. It was divided among his sons and grandsons.

Nero (36–68)

Nero was the most notorious of Roman emperors. During his reign, from 54 to 68, his policy was to kill people at his own caprice. According to the biographer Plutarch, Nero poisoned his stepbrother, had his wife and mother killed, and butchered the children of Roman nobles. He set fire to Rome and prevented the citizens from putting out the flames. Legend has it that Nero "fiddled while Rome burned."

Described as a small man with spotted skin, yellowish hair, and dull gray eyes, Nero was vain and arrogant. His favorite color was purple and he forbade anyone in Rome from wearing anything that shade. He renamed the month April, Neroneus, and changed the name of Rome to Neropolis. After fourteen years of tyranny, the Roman Senate sent army officers to arrest Nero. The emperor was afraid to be punished and afraid to kill himself, so he had his slave take his life.

Pol Pot (1928–   )

Pol Pot, a Communist leader, became prime minister of Cambodia in 1976. His Khmer Rouge regime was responsible for the execution of one million Cambodians. At the hands of Pol Pot another two million Cambodians died from forced labor and starvation. His reign of terror lasted until 1979, when he was overthrown by a Vietnamese invasion. However, he continued to influence the Khmer Rouge regime from his home in the countryside until 1985, when he supposedly retired at the age of fifty-seven. There is some evidence that Pol Pot is still active today.

Spies and Traitors

Benedict Arnold (1741–1801)

Benedict Arnold was an American general who served in the Revolutionary War and achieved many military successes. Arnold felt slighted, however, when he was reprimanded for abusing his authority. In 1780 he plotted to betray the American post at West Point to the British. The information Arnold was sending to the British was captured by the Americans. Arnold escaped to a British ship, and continued to fight for the British against the Americans until the war ended in 1781. He then escaped to England, where he died. He was scorned by both England and America for his traitorous activities. His name has become synonymous with the word traitor.

Brutus (85–42 B.C.)

Marcus Brutus was a Roman politician and soldier. Early in his career he sided with Pompey against Julius Caesar. After Pompey was defeated by Caesar, Brutus was pardoned. But Brutus turned against Caesar once more. After Caesar became emperor, Brutus and a few others plotted his assassination. As Caesar was appearing before the Roman Senate, he was surrounded by assassins holding knives. As he was being stabbed to death Caesar said to Brutus, "Et tu Brute?," which is Latin for "Even you, Brutus?" Brutus was later defeated in battle by some friends of Caesar. After that he committed suicide.

Judas (d. c. A.D. 30)

Judas Iscariot was one of the twelve apostles of Jesus Christ. Judas accepted thirty pieces of silver to lead soldiers to Jesus and identify him with a kiss. As soon as Judas kissed Jesus, the soldiers took Jesus away, and he was tried and hung on a cross to die. Judas is said to have been so overcome with guilt when Jesus died that he committed suicide by hanging himself. The silver accepted by Judas is referred to as "blood money" and was used to buy a potter's field.

Mata Hari (1876–1917)

Margaretha Gertrude Zelle was born and married in Holland. When she left her husband to perform exotic dances on the stages of Europe, she changed her name to

Mata Hari. As a performer she was the friend of several French officials, and she also befriended many Germans in influential positions. When World War I broke out between the Germans on one side and the French and English on the other, Mata Hari was arrested as a spy for the Germans. French authorities jailed her in Paris, and soon thereafter she was ordered to be executed. She refused to wear the customary blindfolds when she met the firing squad. It is said that she even winked at the soldiers before they shot her. Today Mata Hari's name conjures up images of a woman of intrigue and betrayal.

Walker Family (Arthur Walker 1935–   )
(John Walker 1938–   )
(Michael Walker 1963–   )

The Walkers are three American men who were convicted in 1985 of selling naval secrets to the Soviet Union. The ringleader was John Walker, a much-decorated ex-Navy officer who had been working as a detective when he was arrested. His son, Michael, was serving in the U.S. Navy as a seaman. John's brother, Arthur, also an ex-Navy officer, made up the third family member of the spy ring. The three men were found out when John tried to recruit his daughter as a spy while she was serving in the Army. She urged her mother, John's ex-wife, to call the FBI. This tip-off led to the FBI investigation that resulted in the trial and conviction of the three men. John and Arthur are now serving life sentences. Michael Walker is serving a twenty-five-year sentence.

Fictional Villains

Bluebeard

Bluebeard is an evil character from a fairy tale titled "Bluebeard." This murderous villain with an ugly blue beard kills and beheads six wives and stashes their bodies in a closet in his home. After marrying his seventh wife, Fatima, he leaves for a long trip. He gives her the keys to the house but warns her not to open the forbidden closet. Overcome by curiosity, Fatima opens the closet, and Bluebeard discovers she has done so. He tries to kill Fatima, but she is saved by her two brothers.

Bluto

Bluto is the bully who constantly battles Popeye for the love of Olive Oyl in the "Popeye the Sailorman" comic. Popeye is physically outmatched by Bluto, who is six feet eight inches tall, and weighs three hundred and seventy-two pounds. However, Popeye gets instant strength when he eats a can of spinach, and he's able to defeat Bluto every time.

Darth Vader

Darth Vader is the evildoer in the *Star Wars* movie trilogy. As the chief henchman of the evil emperor of the Galaxy, Darth Vader wears black and a full-faced mask. He is a former Jedi warrior who gave himself over to the dark side of the Force. At the climax of the third movie, Darth Vader is instructed to execute his own son, Luke Skywalker, but he's unable to do so. Instead he turns on his own master and kills him before dying himself.

Dracula

Count Dracula of Transylvania is a vampire in the novel *Dracula* by the English author Bram Stoker. By day Dracula is a corpse interred in a cemetery. By night he seeks out human victims and pierces their necks with his fanglike teeth. Once the life blood is sucked from his victims, they, too, become vampires under Dracula's power. Count Dracula is finally put to rest when a wooden stake is driven through his heart.

Fagin

Fagin is the money-hungry leader of a gang of orphaned boys in the Charles Dickens novel *Oliver Twist*. Fagin trains

Oliver Twist and the other boys to pick pockets and steal for him. His evil ways are outmatched only by Bill Sikes, the brutal criminal who is his partner in crime.

Fu Manchu

Fu Manchu first appeared in a magazine serial in England in 1912. He was created by Sax Rohmer and is a scientific genius who tries to conquer the world and set up his own empire. Rohmer describes his villain as the "archangel of evil." Fu Manchu tortures, murders, and poisons anyone who stands in the way of his conquest. Many stories and movies tell his tale.

Medea

Medea is an evil sorceress from Greek myths. Determined to help her loved one, Jason, obtain the Golden Fleece, she betrays her father, has her own brother killed, and she tricks the daughter of one of Jason's enemies into killing her father. Finally, when Jason rejects Medea and marries another woman, she wreaks her final revenge. She sends the new bride a magic gown as a gift. When the bride tries on the dress, it bursts into flames and she is burned to death.

Procrustes

Procrustes is the evil son of Poseidon in Greek mythology. He entices innocent travelers to his home and tortures them by making them fit his special bed. Those who are too short are stretched out to fit. Those who are too tall are made to fit by having their legs lopped off.

Simon Legree

The name Simon Legree has come to be associated with

the evils of slavery. In the novel *Uncle Tom's Cabin* by Harriet Beecher Stowe, Legree is an alcoholic tyrant who oversees the slaves on a Southern plantation. When he buys the slave called Uncle Tom, he is so cruel to him that eventually he beats him to death. Stowe's portrait of Legree provides an important depiction of the abuses suffered by slaves in America.

The Most Infamous Villain of All Time

Satan

Satan is the Devil. He is known as the "Prince of Darkness" and is considered the source of all evil, the opposite of goodness. Satan freely roams the earth, leading people into sin. In both the Old Testament and the New Testament of the Bible, he is man's greatest tempter. When pictured, Satan is often shown with a tail, hooves, horns, and a pointed beard. He wears red and carries a pitchfork.

LOVERS

• •

Lovers may sacrifice more for each other than would just ordinary friends. In our history and literature there are many sad stories about lovers who die of heartbreak because they cannot be together. There are also moving stories of lovers who endure terrible hardships and are finally rewarded with a happy reunion.

Real-Life Lovers

Antony and Cleopatra (c. 82–30 B.C.) (69–30 B.C.)

Cleopatra is known as one of the greatest romantic heroines of history. She was the queen of Egypt, a woman renowned for her intelligence, beauty, and love of luxury. When Mark Antony, a powerful Roman politician, visited Cleopatra in Egypt, he fell deeply in love with her. Cleopatra married Antony in 37 B.C., hoping he would help her restore the power of her kingdom. The Romans were threatened by their union, fearing that together, Antony and Cleopatra planned to rule the Roman Empire. The Romans sent an army to destroy Antony's military forces and defeated them. Soon after the battle, Antony heard false reports that Cleopatra was dead and he tried to kill himself with his sword. He was taken to Cleopatra, and died in her arms. Cleopatra was then imprisoned by the Romans. Filled with grief over the loss of Antony, Cleopatra decided to take her own life.

She was said to have died by allowing an asp (a poisonous snake) to bite her.

Hiawatha and Minnehaha

Hiawatha was a legendary Native American Chief who founded the Iroquois League. The story of his love for Minnehaha is told in the poem "The Song of Hiawatha" by Henry Wadsworth Longfellow. It is difficult to separate truth from fiction, but according to the poem, when Hiawatha journeys to avenge his mother's death, he meets Minnehaha, a young woman from another tribe. The pair fall in love and marry against the wishes of Hiawatha's tribe, who want him to marry within his own tribe. Their love story ends when Minnehaha dies of a fever during a winter famine. Hiawatha is left grieving bitterly over her sudden and early death.

John Alden and Priscilla (c. 1599–1687) (1602–1685)

In 1858 Henry Wadsworth Longfellow published his famous poem "The Courtship of Miles Standish." It is difficult to separate history and invention in the poem, which tells of a romantic triangle between Miles Standish, John Alden, and Priscilla Mullens. The three met aboard the

Mayflower when it sailed for America in 1620. Miles Standish, the military leader of the Plymouth colony, was married but his wife died the first winter. John Alden was single and a good friend of Miles Standish. Eighteen-year-old Priscilla lost her entire family after a few months in America. When Miles Standish decided to remarry, he chose Priscilla to be his wife. Afraid that his proposal would not be eloquent enough, he asked John Alden to propose for him. Priscilla's answer to Alden's passionate proposal was, "Why do you not speak for yourself, John?" In any case it is true that John Alden won the love of Priscilla. They were married in 1622.

Napoleon and Josephine (1769–1821) (1763–1814)

Napoleon Bonaparte was a rising French general when he met and fell in love with Josephine de Beauharnaise, a Creole beauty from Martinique. They seemed an unlikely couple. Josephine was a widow with two children who lived in fashionable French society. Napoleon was unmarried, six years younger, and uncomfortable in social settings. Despite the objections of his family, Napoleon and Josephine married. During their thirteen-year marriage, Napoleon conquered most of Europe and became emperor of France. Josephine remained in Paris, where she socialized and entertained lavishly. In 1810 Napoleon had his marriage to Josephine annulled so he could marry Marie-Louise of Austria. She gave birth to a son, Napoleon II, who could be an heir to Napoleon's throne. Though he was no longer married to Josephine, Napoleon remained devoted and generous to her until her death in 1814.

The Duke and Duchess of Windsor (1894–1972) (1896–1986)

Edward VIII was crowned king of England in 1936. At that time he was in love with Wallis Warfield Simpson, an American woman who was suing her second husband for divorce. Edward insisted on marrying Wallis, but since the law prohibited a divorced woman from becoming queen of England, the British government considered her an unacceptable mate. Edward abdicated his throne saying, "Without the help and support of the woman I love, I cannot carry on as king." His younger brother, George VI, became king, and Edward was named the Duke of Windsor. He married Wallis the following year. Their marriage lasted thirty-five years, until Edward died in 1972. Their love was considered by some to be the "romance of the century."

John Lennon and Yoko Ono (1940–1980) (1933–   )

One of the most famous romances in the history of rock and roll is that of John Lennon and Yoko Ono. Lennon was a singer and songwriter for the Beatles. Ono was a successful performance artist. When they were married in 1969, their honeymoon was a staged media event. John and Yoko stayed in bed in a hotel in Amsterdam, eating brown rice and talking about world peace to an audience of reporters and photographers. Throughout their marriage they combined their creative talents in music, the arts, and on behalf of social causes. After the Beatles split up, John and Yoko performed and recorded together. One of their most famous lyrics is, "All we are saying is, give peace a chance." Their celebrated union ended tragically in 1980, when John was shot and killed by Mark David Chapman, a deranged fan.

Fictional Lovers

Beauty and the Beast

In the French fairy tale "Beauty and the Beast," Beauty is a kind and lovely young girl, and Beast is an ugly, gruff creature. Beauty meets Beast when she is sent to his castle for three months to return a favor for her father. During her stay, Beauty becomes less fearful of Beast. But she misses her father, and one day she asks if she may return home for a visit. Beast agrees, on the condition that she stay only one week. But Beauty can't help staying longer. Then she has a nightmare about Beast's being in danger, so she quickly sets off for the castle. When she finds Beast dying of grief, she realizes she loves him and promises to marry

him. Beast is suddenly released from an evil spell and turns back into the handsome prince he once was. They marry and live happily ever after.

Cupid and Psyche

The story of Cupid and Psyche (SI-kee) is from Roman

mythology. Cupid is a handsome god who falls in love with a young human girl named Psyche. Cupid visits Psyche in the dark of the night so that she will not see his face. One night, Psyche is overcome by curiosity. She lights a lamp to get a glimpse of her lover's face. Cupid awakens and angrily runs away. The two are separated for a long period of time, and Psyche is punished by Cupid's mother. After serving her penance, Psyche is reunited with Cupid. They marry, and Psyche is made a goddess and becomes immortal.

Romeo and Juliet

In 1594 William Shakespeare wrote *Romeo and Juliet*, a play about two young lovers whose lives and love are destroyed by their families. In the play, Romeo Montague is a passionate young man who falls in love with Juliet Capulet. Their romance is forbidden by their families, who are feuding with each other. Romeo and Juliet marry in secret, but their marriage is short-lived. Romeo becomes involved in a fight and kills Juliet's cousin, for which he is banished. While he is gone, Juliet's parents, unaware of her secret marriage, betroth her to another man. In order to avoid the wedding, Juliet drinks a sleeping potion and tricks her family into thinking she is dead. When news of Juliet's supposed death reaches Romeo, he rushes to her tomb. Seeing her apparently lifeless body he kills himself with poison. Juliet awakes from her sleep to find Romeo dead beside her. She then takes her own life. The tragic love story of Romeo and Juliet has been retold many times.

Superman and Lois Lane

Created by Jerry Siegel and Abe Shuster, Superman and Lois Lane are comic-book characters who have been in love for over fifty years. Superman is a crime-fighting hero with superhuman powers. He disguises himself as Clark Kent, a bumbling newspaperman. Lois Lane is a reporter who works with Clark Kent. Unaware that Clark and Superman are the same person, Lois competes with Clark on the job, but is head over heels in love with Superman. Clark Kent loves Lois but is often frustrated that she does not return his affection. In Superman's adventures, his romance with Lois is complicated by rivalry, intrigue, and mixed identities.

Tristan and Isolde

The story of Tristan and Isolde is a medieval legend. Tristan is a handsome young knight who is sent by his uncle, King Mark, to Ireland. His mission is to bring back to England a young woman, Isolde, to marry the king. On the return journey, Tristan and Isolde unknowingly drink a love potion. They fall deeply in love with each other. When they reach England, King Mark learns of their secret love. In anger, he banishes Tristan from his kingdom. As the exiled Tristan lies dying, he sends for Isolde. She arrives too late to save him. Overcome with grief, she lies down beside him and dies of a broken heart.

FRIENDS AND PARTNERS
• •

Comedian Stan Laurel is rarely discussed without a mention of his partner, Oliver Hardy. And who can talk about neat Felix Unger from *The Odd Couple* without bringing up his sloppy roommate, Oscar Madison. Below are some real and fictional duos who together have made themselves memorable.

Real Partners

Marie and Pierre Curie (1867–1934) (1859–1906)

This husband and wife team, the most outstanding couple in science, were married in 1895. Marie Sklodowska Curie was a chemist and physicist from Poland. Pierre Curie was a chemist from France. Together they won the 1903 Nobel Prize in physics for their work in radioactivity. Three years later Pierre was killed in a road accident in Paris. Marie continued to work alone. In 1911 she won a second Nobel Prize in chemistry for the discovery of radium and polonium.

Currier and Ives (1813–1888) (1824–1895)

Nathaniel Currier was a lithographer and seller of prints. He was a tall, gaunt, serious man. J. Merrit Ives was a bookkeeper with a keen artistic eye. He was plump and jovial. In 1857 these two men became business partners. Together, they produced hand-colored prints of events in nineteenth-century American life. Currier and Ives prints were sold all over the U.S. and throughout Europe. When they retired, their sons continued the business until 1907.

Gilbert and Sullivan (1836–1911) (1842–1900)

These two nineteenth-century Englishmen wrote many comic operas. *The Pirates of Penzance* and *HMS Pinafore* are among their still-popular works. William Gilbert wrote the lyrics and dialogue, and Arthur Sullivan wrote the music. Gilbert and Sullivan are known for their satire of the stodgy Victorian society in which they lived.

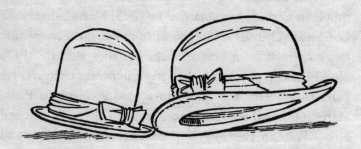

Laurel and Hardy (1890–1965) (1892–1957)

Stan Laurel was born Arthur Jefferson in England. Oliver Hardy was born in Atlanta, Georgia, two years later.

They teamed up when they were in their thirties and formed the first great comedy film team. Wearing derby hats and neckties, they created comedy that was characterized by their always being in each other's way. Laurel was thin and played the part of a skinny, dumb Englishman. Hardy was stout and played the part of a pompous, grouchy, fat American. Laurel and Hardy were one of the most successful and memorable comic duos of all time.

Lewis and Clark (1774–1809) (1770–1838)

Meriwether Lewis and William Clark were both from Virginia. They met while serving in the army in the late 1700s. Later Lewis became the private secretary to President Jefferson. The president asked Lewis to explore the Pacific Northwest, and Lewis asked Clark to be his partner for the expedition. Lewis acted as the doctor and scientist on the journey. Clark, who had frontier experience, was the mapmaker. They were well-matched partners, both making valuable contributions to the success of the expedition, which took place from 1804 to 1806.

Rodgers and Hammerstein (1902–1979) (1895–1960)

Oscar Hammerstein II wrote the words and Richard Rodgers wrote the music. Together for eighteen years, this duo made music history in the twentieth century with such Broadway hits as *Oklahoma!*, *South Pacific*, and *The Sound of Music*. First the partners would talk over the storyline of the show. Hammerstein would then go to his farm in Pennsylvania and write the lyrics. When he was finished, he sent his lyrics to Rodgers, who began composing music to go with the words. Rodgers and Hammerstein are considered the most successful partnership in American theater.

The Wright Brothers (Orville 1871–1948) (Wilbur 1867–1912)

Orville and Wilbur Wright worked together as airplane inventors. Orville was four years younger. As children they showed an early interest in flight—their favorite toy was a homemade helicopter powered by rubber bands. As adults they owned a bicycle shop in Dayton, Ohio, where they spent their spare time working on their airplane, the *Flyer I*. On December 17, 1903, Orville, who won the coin toss to see which brother would do it, became the first to fly a power-driven airplane. Wilbur made the fourth flight of the day and was airborne for fifty-nine seconds. Together these American brothers made aviation history.

Biblical Partners

Adam and Eve

In the Old Testament of the Bible, Adam and Eve were introduced as the first pair of humans. Adam was made from the dust of the earth. God breathed life into him and then created Eve from Adam's rib. Together they lived in great happiness in the Garden of Eden, until they were tempted by Satan, in the form of a snake, to eat forbidden fruit. They were punished by being driven from the Garden of Eden to the world outside. There they gave birth to children and were considered the parents of mankind.

Fictional Partners

Batman and Robin

These two comic-book heroes created by Bob Kane wage a tireless battle against crime from their secret bat cave in Gotham City. In the original story, Batman's real name is Bruce Wayne. As a young boy he witnesses his parents' senseless death at the hands of thugs. He swears vengeance on the criminal underworld and from that moment on, Batman takes years to prepare himself. He studies criminology, martial arts, and acrobatics. When he is ready, he takes on the identity of Batman with a mask, a cape, and a batmobile. Batman is joined by Dick Grayson, a trapeze artist who also witnessed his parents' murder. When Grayson joins Batman, he takes the name Robin, after Robin Hood. Batman and Robin become constant companions in midnight crusades against crime.

Damon and Pythias

The story of Damon and Pythias, two young friends, is from Greek mythology. When Pythias is condemned to death by the tyrant ruler of his city, his last request is to go home to his birthplace to put his affairs in order and say his good-byes. His friend Damon offers to stay in his place and die for him if he does not return, and Pythias is allowed to go. When Pythias is delayed, Damon is ready to die for him. In the nick of time, Pythias returns. The hard heart of the tyrant is softened by this extraordinary show of friendship. He calls off the execution and the two young friends are both saved.

Holmes and Watson

Sherlock Holmes is a well-known detective from nineteenth-century English fiction. Dr. Watson is his trusted and devoted partner in crime solving. They were created by Sir Arthur Conan Doyle, a British physician turned novelist, who wrote sixty detective stories. In these stories, Holmes and Watson live together at 221B Baker Street, in London, during the 1880s and 1890s. Holmes has an exceptional memory and can solve mysteries that seem unsolvable. Watson helps Holmes by taking extensive notes and acting as a sounding board. Together they solve hundreds of criminal cases.

Oscar and Felix

The characters of Oscar Madison and Felix Unger are from a play by Neil Simon called *The Odd Couple*. The play later became a popular TV show.

Oscar is a divorced sportswriter. He takes pity on his friend Felix, a TV news reporter, who has recently separated from his wife. He invites Felix to share his apartment. But Oscar and Felix are extreme opposites. Oscar is a slob who's interested in sports and gambling. He puts ketchup on everything he eats. Felix is compulsively neat. He is interested in such things as opera, commemorative stamps, and fine dining. The two bicker constantly but live together for many years.

R 2-D 2 and C-3PO

These two robot pals are the creation of George Lucas for his film *Star Wars*. In the movie, R2-D2 and C-3PO help Luke Skywalker in his fight against the evil Galactic Empire. R2-D2 and C-3PO are inseparable and complement one another. C-3PO is tall, nervous, sensitive, and speaks

hundreds of languages. R2-D2 is short, fearless, and unthinking. He does not speak, but bleeps. C-3PO often cautions R2-D2 against being too aggressive and having himself destroyed. R2-D2 saves C-3PO, who is often injured. The robots also appear in two sequels, *The Empire Strikes Back* and *Return of the Jedi*, where they continue to battle the evil Empire.

Tom Sawyer and Huck Finn

Tom Sawyer and Huck Finn are the creations of the American author Mark Twain, whose real name was Samuel Clemens. Tom and Huck are best friends. Their many adventures are described in *The Adventures of Tom Sawyer* and *Huckleberry Finn*. Tom is the flamboyant one, a boy whose wild imagination is fueled by the many books he reads. Huck is a decent and honest boy but is treated as a social outcast because his father, "Pap," is the town drunk. The two friends' adventures are often upheld as an example of American boyhood in the nineteenth century.

RIVALS AND FOES
• •

People who compete for the same thing are rivals. People who fight each other are foes. All of these rivals and foes are famous people whose names are linked because of their conflicting desires and ambitions.

Real Rivals and Foes

Amundsen and Scott (1872–1928) (1869–1912)

Roald Amundsen and Robert Scott were polar explorers who each attempted to be the first person to reach the South Pole. Amundsen, a Norwegian, set out with a party of four men and a team of huskies. Scott, an Englishman, traveled with four men and a team of ponies. Amundsen's trip went smoothly. He reached the Pole on December 14, 1911, and left a note for Scott. Scott arrived about a month later on January 17, 1912. His trip had been difficult. His ponies had died on the way, and the men of the expedition had to pull their sleds. Devastated to learn he had been beaten by Amundsen, Scott set out to return to his base camp. But his party was plagued by blizzards. By the end of March, all of the men, including Scott, had died of frostbite and starvation.

Elizabeth and Mary (1533–1603) (1542–1587)

During the sixteenth century, Elizabeth I, a Protestant, was the queen of England. Her cousin Mary was Catholic, and queen of the Scots. The Catholics and Protestants had been vying for control of England ever since Elizabeth's father, Henry VIII, had converted from Catholicism to Protestantism. When Protestant dislike of Mary became intense in Scotland, she fled for her life. Elizabeth gave her refuge in England, where she was kept as a "guest," or prisoner, for nineteen years. Mary and her advisors plotted countless times to remove Elizabeth from the throne. Finally, in 1587, Parliament found Mary guilty of treason and condemned her to death. Elizabeth was troubled by the act but finally signed the papers for execution. Mary was executed and the rivalry was ended.

Hamilton and Burr (1755–1804) (1756–1836)

On July 11, 1804, two prominent American politicians faced each other in a duel. They were Alexander Hamilton, the first U.S. secretary of the treasury, and Aaron Burr, a political leader. Burr tied with Thomas Jefferson in the 1800 presidential election. Because of Hamilton he was made vice president instead of president. Later, when Burr ran for governor of New York, he lost, blaming his loss on negative remarks made by Hamilton. He then challenged Hamilton to a duel. Hamilton accepted the challenge, even though he was against dueling. (His son had died in a duel a few years earlier.) On the fateful day of the duel, Hamilton faced Burr. Hamilton shot into the air rather than at his foe. Burr's shot hit Hamilton, and he died the following day.

Hatfields and McCoys

These two names are synonymous with rivalry. The story of their feud has been told in comic strips, songs, movies, and television shows. The Hatfields and the McCoys were two families who lived near each other on the banks of the Big Sandy River. The Hatfields lived on the West Virginia side of the river. The McCoys lived on the Kentucky side. The feud between them began during the Civil War when the families were on opposing sides. It heated up in 1878 during a dispute over a hog. In 1882 a Hatfield tried to elope with a McCoy, and the rivalry became violent. The feud lasted twelve years. Eighty people were involved and twelve of them were killed in the fighting.

Legendary Rivals and Foes

Bond and Blofeld

Bond and Blofeld are characters in Ian Fleming's novels. James Bond is an agent who works for the British Secret Service. Ernst Stavro Blofeld is head of an international gang of terrorists, called SPECTRE (Special Executive for Counterintelligence, Terrorism, Revenge, and Extortion). In three novels and seven films, Bond battles Blofeld. Blofeld is a brilliant criminal who is determined to take control of the world by instigating World War III. Bond is finally able to capture him and save the world.

Capulets and Montagues

The Capulets and Montagues are two feuding families in William Shakespeare's play *Romeo and Juliet*. Juliet Capulet and Romeo Montague are deeply in love. But because of their families' rivalry, they marry in secret. A fight takes place among the young men in the families, and after a series of miscommunications, both Romeo and Juliet take their own lives. The tragic deaths of Romeo and Juliet cause the two families to reconcile.

Robin Hood and the Sheriff of Nottingham

The legend of Robin Hood dates back to the twelfth century and takes place in Sherwood Forest, England. Robin and his band of outlaws, the Merry Men, rob from the rich to give to poor widows and orphans. Robin's enemy is the sheriff of Nottingham, a powerful and close ally of the cruel Prince John. Robin Hood and the sheriff of Nottingham fight many battles both in Nottingham and in Sherwood Forest. For years the sheriff tries to capture Robin Hood. The rivalry ends when the sheriff is killed in a fight. The good King Richard then returns to England and takes his throne back from Prince John. Robin is proclaimed a hero by the king.

Romulus and Remus

According to Roman mythology, Romulus and Remus were twin brothers who founded the city of Rome. At birth they were thrown into the Tiber River. When they were washed ashore, a she-wolf found and raised them. As young men they decided to build a new city. However, they could not agree where the city should be built. To settle the argument the two brothers agreed that the one who saw the most vultures on a given day should choose the site. Romulus claimed he'd seen twelve vultures. Remus, who'd seen only six, thought his brother had cheated. They quarreled and Romulus killed Remus.

Biblical Rivals and Foes

Cain and Abel

The story of Cain and Abel is from the Old Testament of the Bible. Cain and Abel are the two sons of Adam and

Eve. Cain, the oldest son, is a farmer who works the soil. Abel, the younger, raises sheep. When they make offerings of their labors to God, God prefers Abel's sheep. Angry and jealous, Cain kills his brother Abel. It is the first murder of humankind. God punishes Cain by sending him out into the land of Nod.

David and Goliath

The story of David and Goliath is from the Old Testament. Goliath, a giant of a man, is a Philistine (FIL-ə-steen). David, a young shepherd boy, is an Israelite. The Philistines and Israelites are at war. When neither side is able to win, Goliath issues a challenge. He asks the Israelites to send one man to fight him. The winner's nation will be the conqueror. Young David is the only Israelite brave enough to take up the challenge. Armed with only a slingshot and five stones he confronts the giant Goliath. David's first shot hits Goliath in the forehead and kills him. The Philistines run and the Israelites pursue and kill them. The Israelites are proclaimed the victors.

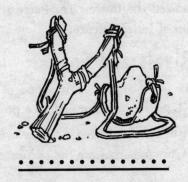

• • • • • • • • • • • • •

SAME NAME PEOPLE

Many people in our history and culture have the same last name. Here's a list of some same name people that will help you keep their identities straight.

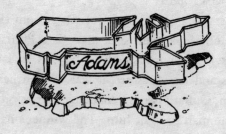

Adams and Adams

Samuel Adams (1722–1803) was an American patriot and speechmaker who helped spark the American Revolution. He organized the Boston Tea Party and later signed the Declaration of Independence.

John Adams (1735–1826) was one of the founding fathers of the U.S. He was the first vice president and the second president of the U.S.

John Quincy Adams (1767–1848) was the son of John Adams. He was also a U.S. president. He was the sixth president, serving after James Monroe.

Abigail Smith Adams (1744–1818) was the second First Lady in American history. She was married to John Adams, the second president of the U.S., and she was the mother of John Quincy Adams, the sixth president of the U.S. Abigail Adams spoke out for the rights of women to be educated and to vote, long before it was acceptable.

Jane Addams (1860–1935) was an American social worker who started Hull House in Chicago, which served the neighborhood poor. She devoted her life to working for peace and for women's rights. In 1931 she was awarded the Nobel Peace Prize.

Barrymore

Ethel Barrymore (1879–1959) was an actress who was considered the "First Lady of American Theater" from the 1900s to the 1940s. She was from a famous acting family that included her brothers Lionel and John, both distinguished actors. A theater on Broadway in New York is named after Ethel Barrymore.

Drew Barrymore (1975–   ) is an American actress known for her parts in movies such as *E.T. The Extra-Terrestrial* (1982) and *Firestarter* (1984). She is the granddaughter of the great actor John Barrymore, and the daughter of John Barrymore, Jr.

Becket and Beckett

Thomas à Becket (c. 1118–1170) was a twelfth-century English clergyman. He was named archbishop of Canterbury, the highest position of the English church. Although he was a friend of King Henry II, the two disagreed on the areas of power of the church and of the king. Four of the king's men murdered Becket in his cathedral.

Samuel Beckett (1906–1989) was a twentieth-century Irish playwright and novelist who lived most of his life in Paris. Beckett won the Nobel Prize for literature in 1969. He wrote plays and novels that portray the absurdities of life. One of his most famous plays is *Waiting for Godot*.

Blackwell

Elizabeth Blackwell (1821–1920) was the first woman in the U.S. to become a doctor. She helped to found the

New York Infirmary for Women and Children and its Women's Medical College.

Antoinette Blackwell (1825–1921) was the first woman in the U.S. to be ordained a Christian minister. She was also one of the first women to receive a college education.

Booth

William Booth (1829–1912) was an Englishman who founded the Salvation Army. The Salvation Army is a Protestant denomination known for its work to help the poor and homeless.

Edwin Thomas Booth (1833–1893) was the older brother of John Wilkes Booth. He was a great Shakespearean actor whose career ended after his brother assassinated President Lincoln. He was elected to the Hall of Fame for Great Americans for his contributions as an actor.

John Wilkes Booth (1838–1865) was an actor who was fanatically dedicated to the Confederacy during the U.S. Civil War. On April 14, 1865, he shot President Abraham

Lincoln, who was attending a performance at Ford's Theater. Booth escaped after the murder but was later found in a barn where he died of gunshot wounds.

Bradley

Milton Bradley (1836–1911) created a board game, "The Checkered Game of Life," in 1860. The game was so successful that he founded Milton Bradley and Company, a toy and game company that still exists today.

Omar Bradley (1893–1981) was a general in the U.S. Army during World War II. He led U.S. troops in the Normandy invasion. Later, President Harry S. Truman named him chairman of the Joint Chiefs of Staff.

Thomas Bradley (1917–   ) is a lawyer and former Los Angeles policeman. He entered politics and in 1973 was elected mayor of Los Angeles.

Bill Bradley (1943–   ) was a Rhodes scholar who played professional basketball for the New York Knickerbockers. In 1979 he was elected to the U.S. Senate as a Democrat from New Jersey.

Brown

Paul Brown (1908–   ) coached the Cleveland Browns football team from 1946 to 1962, then coached the Cincinnati Bengals from 1968 to 1976. He is a member of the Pro Football Hall of Fame.

James Brown (1928–   ) is known as the "godfather of soul." As the originator of funk and rap music, he is one of the most influential artists in black music history.

Jim Brown (1936–   ) was a fullback for the Cleveland Browns who was named NFL Player of the Year in 1958 and in 1963. After retiring from football he took up acting, mainly in action movies.

Holmes

Oliver Wendell Holmes (1809–1894) was an American poet and essayist. His most famous poems include "Old Ironsides" and "The Chambered Nautilus." He was elected to the Hall of Fame for Great Americans.

Oliver Wendell Holmes, Jr. (1841–1935) was the son of Oliver Wendell Holmes. He distinguished himself as a jurist and associate justice of the U.S. Supreme Court.

Like his father, he was elected to the Hall of Fame for Great Americans.

Larry Holmes (1949–   ) was the World Boxing Council heavyweight champ in 1978. He defeated Ken Norton for the title.

Horne

Lena Horne (1917–   ) is an American singer who has performed in nightclubs, on TV, in movies, and in many musicals.

Marilyn Horne (1934–   ) is an American opera singer. She is a mezzo-soprano who is known for the power of her voice. Marilyn Horne has performed in most of the famous opera houses in the world.

Jackson

Andrew Jackson (1767–1845) was the seventh president of the United States. In the War of 1812 he won a military victory at New Orleans. His nickname was "Old Hickory" because he was thought to be as hard and tough as a hickory tree.

Thomas Jackson (1824–1863) was a Confederate army general. After the first battle of Bull Run, he earned the nickname "Stonewall Jackson" for his brave stand against Union troops.

Mahalia Jackson (1911–1972) was a black American singer who became internationally famous for her gospel singing. She began singing in churches, then went on to record and perform throughout the world.

Jesse Jackson (1941–   ) is a Baptist clergyman who became a civil rights leader and politician. In 1984 and 1988 he ran for the Democratic nomination for U.S. president.

Reggie Jackson (1946–   ) is a U.S. baseball player who led the American League in home runs in 1973 and 1975. He played the position of outfield for a number of teams, including the Oakland Athletics, the Baltimore Orioles, and the New York Yankees.

Michael Jackson (1958–   ) is a musical sensation who began singing with his brothers when he was five years old. They called themselves The Jackson Five. Michael Jackson later went on to become one of the most successful solo rock and roll performers and teenage idols in music history.

Janet Jackson (1966–   ) is an American pop singer, and the sister of Michael Jackson. She signed her first recording contract at the age of sixteen and was later nominated for several Grammies for her solo album *Control*.

Johnson

Andrew Johnson (1808–1875) became the seventeenth president of the U.S. when Abraham Lincoln was assassinated. While president, he was impeached on charges of corruption. He was acquitted in the Senate, so he remained in office though he was politically powerless.

Lyndon B. Johnson (1908–1973) became the thirty-sixth president of the U.S. when he succeeded the assassinated President John Kennedy. He was known for his great political skill and ability to have legislation passed by Congress.

Jones

John Paul Jones (1747–1792) was an American naval hero. When he was asked to surrender during a battle of the Revolution, his famous reply was, "Sir, I have not yet begun to fight."

James Earl Jones (1931–   ) is an American actor best known for his stage performances. He won a Tony award for his performance in *The Great White Hope*. He is the voice of Darth Vader in *Star Wars*. In recent years he has acted in films such as *Field of Dreams*.

Strauss

Johann Strauss (the younger) (1825–1899) was an Austrian composer known for his dance music and several operettas. He was dubbed "The Waltz King."

Richard Strauss (1864–1949) was a German composer. He wrote many operas, including *Der Rosenkavalier* and *Salome*.

Turner

Lana Turner (1920–   ) is an American film star. Her first movie was *Love Finds Andy Hardy* (1938). She was known as the original "sweater girl."

Tina Turner (1941–   ) is a rock and soul singer who first achieved fame with the man who was then her husband, Ike Turner, in the Ike and Tina Turner Revue. She is now a solo performer and recording artist.

Webster

Noah Webster (1758–1843) was a writer who Americanized the English language with his *American Spelling Book*. He used American spelling rather than British spelling. As a result words such as colour were written color. In 1828 he wrote the *American Dictionary of the English Language*.

Daniel Webster (1782–1852) was a lawyer, U.S. congressman, senator, presidential candidate, and U.S. secretary of state. He was known as the great orator of his time.

SECTION II:

PLACES TO KNOW

In this section you will find some famous and familiar places in the world. There are fantasy worlds such as Brigadoon and real addresses such as 221B Baker Street. You will also find places that once thrived but are now lost. There are famous routes to travel, streets to walk, and foods named after places. And, if you've ever wondered what happened to places such as Persia or the Belgian Congo, you'll learn that they still exist in the world, but their names have changed.

. . . .

FAMOUS ADDRESSES

Some street addresses become even better known than the people who live there. An address is often important because it is the residence of a celebrity or politician, or because it's where a significant event happened. Here are some famous addresses:

10 Downing Street, London, England, is the official residence of the British prime minister. It is presently occupied by John Major.

13 Rue Madeleine, Le Havre, France, was Gestapo headquarters in the 1946 movie of the same name.

17 Cherry Tree Lane, London, England, is the address of the Banks family in the 1964 movie *Mary Poppins*.

221B Baker Street, London, England, is the residence of detective Sherlock Holmes.

263 Princengracht, Amsterdam, Netherlands, is where Anne Frank and her family hid from the Nazis during World War II.

1313 Mockingbird Lane is the home of the TV family the Munsters.

1600 Pennsylvania Avenue, Washington, D.C., is the official residence of the president of the United States.

AREAS OF THE WORLD

· ·

Have you ever wondered what was behind the iron curtain? Which of the seven continents is "the continent"? Where is the sunbelt? Here are some of the areas of the world you won't find on a map.

Bermuda Triangle

An area in the Atlantic Ocean bounded by Florida, Puerto Rico, and Bermuda Island. Storms are common in this area and a number of aircraft and ships have disappeared from here.

Bible Belt

A population of the U.S. who are religious fundamentalists (people who interpret the Bible literally) and live primarily in the southeastern and midwestern parts of the country.

"The Continent"

Europe is commonly called "the Continent" by the British. The other continents are Antarctica, Africa, Asia, Australia, North America, and South America.

Iron Curtain

The iron curtain was a term used to describe the division between Western and Eastern Europe before the sweeping political changes in the late 1980s. The countries behind the iron curtain were those under Communist rule: Albania, Bulgaria, Czechoslovakia, East Germany, Hungary, Poland, Romania.

Land Down Under

The land down under refers to the continent of Australia because of its location in the Southern Hemisphere.

Low Countries

Because these European countries are near sea level, they are called the low countries. They are Belgium, Luxembourg, and the Netherlands.

New World

This refers to the Western Hemisphere of the world. It is a land mass that includes North America and South America. It was considered to be "new" by Europeans when they first started traveling to it.

Old World

The Old World refers to the Eastern Hemisphere of the world, particularly Europe. After their discovery of America, Europeans referred to their part of the world as "old."

Orient

The word orient means east. The Orient refers to Asia, especially China and Japan.

Sea of Tranquility

This is the area of the moon chosen for the first moon landing by humans. It was thought to be similar to the desert areas of the U.S.

Silicon Valley

This is an area of the Santa Clara Valley in northern California known for its many high-technology companies. This nickname comes from the wafers made of silicon that are used in computer technology.

Sunbelt

This is an area of the South and Southwest known for its warm, sunny climate. The states include Alabama, Arizona, Florida, Georgia, Virginia, North Carolina, South Carolina, and Texas.

Third World

This refers to countries of the world that are not aligned with either the United States or the Soviet Union. It also designates these countries as developing countries. Third world countries are primarily in Africa, Asia, and South America.

BALLPARKS AND
THEIR HOME TEAMS

E very ballpark in the United States and Canada has its own character. Fenway Park in Boston is small and cozy. Yankee Stadium in New York is steeped in tradition. Here are the names and locations of the major league stadiums and what makes them unique.

Name	Location	Team
Anaheim Stadium Known as the Big "A"	Anaheim, CA	California Angels
Arlington Stadium Scoreboard shaped like the state of Texas	Arlington, TX	Texas Rangers
Astrodome First domed stadium	Houston, TX	Houston Astros
Atlanta-Fulton County Stadium Hank Aaron hit his 715th home run here, breaking Babe Ruth's home run record	Atlanta, GA	Atlanta Braves
Busch Memorial Stadium Located at waterfront adjacent to the symbolic Gateway Arch	St. Louis, MO	St. Louis Cardinals

Name	Location	Team
Candlestick Park The only ballpark where a game was cancelled due to an earthquake, October 1989	San Francisco, CA	San Francisco Giants
Cleveland Municipal Stadium Bowl-shaped stadium on the shores of Lake Erie	Cleveland, OH	Cleveland Indians
Comiskey Park Was oldest major league ballpark still in active use until 1991 season, when a new Comiskey Park was completed	Chicago, IL	Chicago White Sox
County Stadium Widely recognized as having best ballpark food	Milwaukee, WI	Milwaukee Brewers
Dodger Stadium Fans rent seat cushions at each game and then toss them onto field after game	Los Angeles, CA	L.A. Dodgers
Fenway Park It opened the day the *Titanic* sunk, 1915	Boston, MA	Boston Red Sox
Hubert H. Humphrey Metrodome Scene of first indoor World Series	Minneapolis, MN	Minnesota Twins

Name	Location	Team
Kingdome First covered stadium on the West Coast	Seattle, WA	Seattle Mariners
Memorial Stadium Place where double dogs (two hot dogs on one bun) were first served	Baltimore, MD	Baltimore Orioles
Jack Murphy Stadium Infield has baseball's most beautiful grass with checkerboard light and dark squares	San Diego, CA	San Diego Padres
Oakland-Alameda County Coliseum Has largest foul territory area	Oakland, CA	Oakland Athletics
Olympic Stadium Only ballpark to have scoreboard and public address system in two languages—French and English	Montreal, Canada	Montreal Expos
Riverfront Stadium First synthetic turf field with cut-out dirt around bases	Cincinnati, OH	Cincinnati Reds
Royals Stadium Has waterjets, artificial turf, and a scoreboard 12 stories high	Kansas City, MO	Kansas City Royals

Name	Location	Team
Shea Stadium Computer-operated scoreboard installed in 1988. Is capable of automatic update of all major league games in progress	Queens, NY	New York Mets
Skydome Opened during 1989 season. Only ballpark with retractable roof. Games can be played indoors or outdoors	Toronto, Canada	Toronto Blue Jays
Three Rivers Stadium Located at confluence of the Ohio, Allegheny, and Monongahela rivers	Pittsburgh, PA	Pittsburgh Pirates
Tiger Stadium Deepest center field	Detroit, MI	Detroit Tigers
Veterans Stadium Largest capacity (62,382) of any National League ballpark	Philadelphia, PA	Philadelphia Phillies
Wrigley Field Ivy-covered walls; last to use lights, 1988	Chicago, IL	Chicago Cubs
Yankee Stadium Has monuments in center field honoring great Yankees of the past	Bronx, NY	New York Yankees

CELEBRATED STREETS

The streets that follow are more than simple thoroughfares. Some of these world-famous streets have been the subject of songs and movies. Some have become synonymous with the business that is located on the street. Have you ever walked down any of these famous streets?

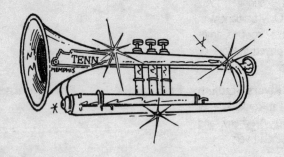

Beale Street

Beale Street is the subject of the song "Beale Street Blues," composed by William C. Handy in 1960. It is a real street in Memphis, Tennessee. Beale Street is lined with clubs where blues music is played.

Broadway

This famous street runs the length of Manhattan Island in New York City. The principal theater district of New York is located on or near Broadway and Forty-second Street. Broadway has come to mean theater.

Champs Élysée

A wide boulevard in Paris, France, noted for its cafés, boutiques, and theaters. It is often regarded as the center of Parisian nightlife.

Fleet Street

This is a street in central London, England. Many newspaper publishers are located on Fleet Street. The street has come to represent British journalism.

Hollywood and Vine

In the heart of the Hollywood section of Los Angeles is an intersection called Hollywood and Vine. At one time it was considered the hub of Hollywood activity, a place where stars and movie moguls could be seen walking or riding in limousines.

Madison Avenue

This street runs from south to north on the East Side of New York City. It is associated with the American advertising business because of all the offices located there.

Rodeo Drive

Pronounced roh-DAY-oh, this is a three-block-long street in Beverly Hills, California. It is famous for its elegant and expensive shops.

Savile Row

A London street that has become synonymous with the best in men's tailoring.

Sesame Street

This is the home of Big Bird, Bert and Ernie, and the rest of the television gang that teach preschool children their letters and numbers. There is no actual Sesame Street except in the television studio in New York City where *Sesame Street* is filmed.

Shubert Alley

This is a private alley in New York City's theater district (between West Forty-fourth and West Forty-fifth streets), where actors once paced and waited word from the powerful theater producers, the Shubert brothers, for jobs.

Skid Row

A run-down district in any city that is frequented by derelicts. The original "Skid Row" was in Seattle.

Sunset Strip

Sunset Boulevard stretches from West Hollywood through Beverly Hills in Los Angeles, California. In the 1960s, songs, movies, and TV shows portrayed a section of Sunset Boulevard known as Sunset Strip as a place where teenagers could be seen driving convertibles and having fun.

Tin Pan Alley

This is not a real street but a reference to the music industry in the U.S. The term is also used to refer to money-making musicians who don't care much about the quality of their music.

Via Dolorosa

This road in Jerusalem is also known as the Anguished Way. It is the road Christ traveled with the cross.

Wall Street

Wall Street is located in lower Manhattan. It was once the site of a wall that protected early settlers. Today it is in the heart of the financial district and its name is synonymous with the U.S. economy.

FAMOUS AMERICAN ROUTES

•••••••••••••••••••••••••••••••••••••

Below is a list of some famous routes in America. Some were originally created to make traveling and trade easier, while others were used so people could escape the bonds of slavery. Though the dirt roads have since been paved, some travel routes established over three hundred years ago for horse and carriage are still used today.

Boston Post Road

The Boston Post Road was laid out in 1672 to make coach travel from New York to Boston speedier. Famous in colonial times, it ran first from Boston to New York, then through New York to Philadelphia, the three largest cities of that time. Today it is also known as Route 1.

Chisolm Trail

The Chisolm Trail was named after Jesse Chisolm, who created the trail by carting buffalo hides over it. In the late 1800s it was used as a cow trail for cattle being herded from San Antonio, Texas, to railways in Kansas.

El Camino Real

El Camino Real was the name of a road in sixteenth-century Spain. It was also the name of the royal highway of the Spanish conquistadors in North America. This road ran through the Spanish settlements in southern California and Mexico in the late 1700s and early 1800s.

Oregon Trail

The Oregon Trail stretched 2,000 miles from Independence, Missouri, across the Rocky Mountains to the Oregon Territory. It was the primary northern route for western settlers. For those traveling by wagon train, the trip over the Oregon Trail took about six months.

Pony Express

From April 1860 to October 1861, mail was carried across the U.S. by horseback riders who relayed it from one to the other. The route for pony express riders was 2,000 miles, and stretched from St. Joseph, Missouri, to Sacramento, California. It took approximately eight days for one bag of mail to cover the distance.

Route 66

From the 1920s to the early 1960s American tourists traveled Route 66 by car to see the heartland of America. Starting in Chicago and reaching to California, Route 66 was at one time considered the main street of America. Its 2,000 miles were dotted with roadside wonders. Route 66 also generated John Steinbeck's Pulitzer Prize–winning novel, *The Grapes of Wrath*, as well as the popular song "Get Your Kicks on Route 66." In 1984 the road was completely phased out by the federal government and replaced with a network of superhighways.

Santa Fe Trail

This was a caravan route for traders in the mid 1800s. It covered 780 miles from Independence, Missouri, to Santa Fe, New Mexico. The trip took from 49 to 60 days. In 1880 the new Santa Fe Railroad eclipsed the trail.

Tobacco Road

The meandering roads of Southern states that were used for rolling barrels of tobacco were called tobacco roads. The roads were built so that tobacco could be rolled from the plantation where it was grown to the inspection stations.

The tobacco road that ran through northern Georgia was the most famous. It is the Tobacco Road referred to in stories, plays, and songs.

Trail of Tears

In the winter of 1838–1839, more than 13,000 members of the Cherokee nation were forced to leave their homeland in the eastern U.S. They were escorted by U.S. Army troops to Indian territory west of the Mississippi River. The 800-mile route they took became known as the Trail of Tears. Some 4,000 people, mostly children and elderly people, died along the Trail of Tears.

Underground Railroad

Before the Civil War, slaves escaped from the South to the northern states and Canada along the Underground Railroad. It actually was neither a railroad nor did it travel underground. Instead the Underground Railroad was a network of houses, barns, and other places where slaves were hidden as they made their way north to freedom.

Wilderness Road

From 1790 to 1840 the Wilderness Road was a main route of western migration of settlers. The trail extended from Virginia through the Cumberland Gap to the Ohio River. It was blazed by Daniel Boone, the famed frontiersman.

FOODS NAMED AFTER PLACES
• •

Baloney

This smoked sausage of beef, veal, and pork is named after its place of origin, Bologna, Italy. Baloney and bologna are varied spellings of the same sausage.

Boston Baked Beans

Boston baked beans originated with the Puritan settlers in New England. Because cooking was forbidden on the Sabbath, a pot of beans was prepared on Saturday evening and set to cook slowly all night long. The beans were served with brown bread on Sunday after church services.

Buffalo Wings

These spicy barbecued chicken wings originated in Buffalo, New York, at the Anchor Bar. Owners Frank and Theresa Bellisimo started a tradition of serving their special chicken wings in hot peppery sauce, accompanied by celery sticks and bleu cheese dressing, on Friday nights. Buffalo wings named after the city, not the bison, are now popular throughout the country.

Frankfurter

Wienerwurst, or Vienna sausage, was first made in Vienna, Austria. Later the same sausage was called a frankfurter after Frankfurt, Germany. Americans were the first to put the wiener or frankfurter on a bun. It was also in the U.S. that these popular sausages were first called hot dogs.

Hamburger

The people of Hamburg, Germany, were the first to cook patties of ground meat. The Hamburg steak was brought to the U.S. by German immigrants. It was Americanized when it was served on a bun and called a hamburger.

Key Lime Pie

This popular dessert was created in the Florida Keys.

An authentic key lime pie is made with the small limes that are grown in these islets off the coast of Florida. The limes are yellow, not green, in color.

Smithfield Ham

The best-known ham in America has been cured in Smithfield, Virginia, for over 350 years. Originally the pigs were fed on peanuts to give the ham its unique flavor. Today the famed hams are cured for over six months to obtain their distinctive taste.

Tabasco Sauce

The red peppers used in making tabasco sauce were brought from Tabasco, Mexico, by a soldier of the Mexican War. The seeds were planted in a flower garden on a Louisiana plantation because of the plant's bright blossoms. A resourceful cook used the red peppers in making a hot sauce. Soon after the end of the Civil War, the family who owned the plantation bottled and sold the sauce for income.

HOMES

• •

A home often reflects its owner. Sometimes we associate our favorite characters from literature with their special homes. Splendid mansions, such as San Simeon, can tell us how wealthy businessmen lived. Other residences, such as Camp David, are important to know about because they're where world leaders gather to make crucial decisions.

Storybook homes

Green Gables

This is the name of a farm located in Avonlea, a fictitious community on Prince Edward Island, Canada. It is the setting of the stories written by L. M. Montgomery about Anne Shirley, an orphan, who is mistakenly sent to Green Gables to live with Matthew and Marilla Cuthbert. The couple is surprised to see Anne because they were expecting a boy. Anne stays on and grows up at Green Gables.

Green Knowe

This old English manor house served as the setting for many of L. M. Boston's children's books. In *The Children of Green Knowe*, the first in the series, Tolly, the main character, visits his great-grandmother and learns all about his relatives who grew up at Green Knowe in the seventeenth century.

House of the Seven Gables

This is the ancestral home of the Pyncheon family in Nathaniel Hawthorne's 1851 novel, *The House of the Seven Gables*. In the story, the dilapidated mansion in Salem, Massachusetts, is under a curse. Eventually the House of the Seven Gables is freed of the curse.

Sunnybrook Farm

In the 1903 novel by Kate Douglas Wiggin, *Rebecca of Sunnybrook Farm*, Rebecca Rowena Randall is sent across the state of Maine to live with her two unmarried aunts on Sunnybrook Farm. Rebecca is a spirited character who is often described as the nicest child in American literature.

Tara

Tara is the name of the O'Hara family estate in the book *Gone With the Wind*, by Margaret Mitchell. In the story, Scarlett O'Hara tries to restore Tara, after it is destroyed during the Civil War. She achieves her goal, but at the cost of losing everything else: money, security, and the love of her husband, Rhett Butler.

Real Residences

Blair House is a guest house used by the president of the United States for visiting heads of state. Located in Washington, D.C., it was built in 1824 and actually consists of four contiguous houses. Blair House is located on Pennsylvania Avenue next to the White House.

Buckingham Palace is located in London, England. It has been the residence of British sovereigns from 1837 to the present. Today it is the home of Queen Elizabeth and Prince Philip. The palace has nearly 600 rooms.

Camp David is the U.S. presidential retreat in the Catoctin Mountains of Maryland. It is a 143-acre compound with more than a dozen buildings. The presidential house is called Aspen Lodge and is a place of total seclusion. It has been used more than twenty times for peace talks between American presidents and foreign chiefs of state.

Chelsea Hotel is a New York City literary landmark. It

has been home to famous authors such as Thomas Wolfe, Mark Twain, O. Henry, and artist Andy Warhol. Sid Vicious, a star of the rock band the Sex Pistols, killed his girlfriend, Nancy, there.

Dakota Apartments are located at Seventy-second Street and Central Park West in New York City. At this site one of the Beatles, John Lennon, lived with his wife, Yoko Ono. He was murdered in the courtyard outside the apartments.

Graceland was Elvis Presley's home located in Whitehaven, a suburb of Memphis, Tennessee. The twenty-three-room mansion is set on 13.8 acres. In front of the house are large white iron gates adorned with musical notes and two green guitars.

Hotel Metropole, in Chicago, Illinois, was the place where mobster Al Capone lived during the 1930s when he was the head of the mob.

Ioloni Palace is the only standing one-time royal residence in the United States. It was the royal residence of King Kalakaua and Queen Kapiolani. Located in Honolulu, Hawaii, it is now a museum, and still contains their elaborate thrones.

Monticello was the home of Thomas Jefferson. He designed and built the house. Its unique features include a revolving desk and an enclosed bed. Monticello is located near Charlottesville, Virginia.

Mount Vernon in Virginia was the home of George Washington. He inherited the mansion when his brother died in 1753. It was built on the banks of the Potomac River.

Sagamore Hill was the home of Teddy Roosevelt. It is located in Oyster Bay, on Long Island, New York. During his presidency it served as a summer White House.

San Simeon, in San Simeon, California, is also known as Hearst's Castle. William Randolph Hearst was a newspaper mogul. His home is considered by many to be the twentieth century's most lavish and ostentatious residence.

Springwood was the home of Franklin Delano Roosevelt at Hyde Park, New York. Roosevelt was born there, and he and his wife, Eleanor, are both buried there. During his twelve years as president of the United States, FDR returned home to Hyde Park more than 200 times, entertaining heads of state.

LEGENDARY PLACES

• •

Many great storytellers have created places for us to travel to with our imaginations. Some of them are described so vividly that it may even seem as if they're real places. Below are some of the most unforgettable places from story and myth.

Atlantis

Atlantis is the lost continent first described by Plato, a Greek philosopher who lived in the fourth century B.C. According to legend, Atlantis was the home of a perfect society where industry and art prospered in 9,560 B.C. After an earthquake Atlantis fell into the Atlantic Ocean and was lost.

Brigadoon

Brigadoon is a magical village in the Scottish highlands. It's been cast under a spell that keeps the entire village asleep except for one day every hundred years. Entry to and exit from the village is limited to a single span bridge. It is said that if anyone ever leaves the village the spell will be broken. The story is told in the 1947 musical *Brigadoon*, and the 1955 movie of the same name.

Camelot

The story of Camelot and King Arthur is told by Thomas Malory in *Le Morte D'Arthur*, and by Alfred Lord Tennyson in "Idylls of the King." In the legend Camelot is the capital of the legendary King Arthur's kingdom, Logres. The city of Camelot is made up of small, thatched houses on the banks of the Camelot River. A huge castle sits on a hill above the village. The main hall of the castle is decorated with mystical symbols and was built by Merlin, the magician. King Arthur's famous round table, which seats his 150 knights, can be found in the castle.

Crusoe's Island

This island is described by Daniel Defoe in *The Life and Surprising Adventure of Robinson Crusoe*. Speranza is the

name of the island on which Robinson Crusoe lands when he is shipwrecked in 1659. It is located in the Atlantic Ocean off the coast of South Africa. No wild beasts occupy the island, although there is plenty of wildlife. Many varied birds and turtles exist on Speranza, and sugar cane and citrus trees thrive there.

Death Star

This gigantic battle station located in space is the flagship of the evil Empire in the George Lucas film *Star Wars*. The Death Star is finally destroyed in battle.

El Dorado

A legendary kingdom located in South America, somewhere near Peru. This capital city, said to be built by the Incas, was made entirely of gold. There was so much gold in El Dorado that the people valued food more. El Dorado was described by Sir Walter Raleigh in his 1596 writings.

Krypton

This distant planet was the birthplace of Superman (or Kal-El, as he was known there), the comic-book hero. Because the planet was dying, Superman's parents sent him into space to save his life. On Earth he was adopted by the Kents and became Clark Kent. His super powers can be diminished only by kryptonite, a radioactive element that affects life-forms native to the planet Krypton. Prolonged exposure to green kryptonite, for example, can cause blood poisoning and, eventually, death.

Lilliput

Lilliput is one of the unforgettable places described in *Gulliver's Travels*, a story by Jonathan Swift. In 1699, Lemuel Gulliver, a surgeon on a merchant ship, is shipwrecked on the island of Lilliput. Gulliver, an average-sized man, seems like a giant on this island, where the inhabitants average less than six inches in height. Lilliput is located somewhere south of Sumatra (Indonesia).

Middle Earth

Somewhere in the northwestern part of the known world lies the fantastic land and creatures of the Middle Earth as described by J.R.R. Tolkien in *The Hobbit*, *The Lord of the Rings*, and other books. In the Middle Earth created by Tolkien, there are men, elves, dwarfs, and hobbits who have special languages and unique histories.

Narnia

Narnia is described in *The Chronicles of Narnia* by C. S. Lewis. In Lewis's tales the land of Narnia was created by

Aslan, a great lion, who came from a country beyond the end of the world. Narnia lies between mountain ranges and is inhabited by dryads, centaurs, fauns, and a witch. Entry to Narnia is either through a wardrobe, by magic rings, or by the power of Aslan. Once in Narnia, one has no idea of the passing of time. But no matter how long one visits, one always returns to the real world a moment after having left it.

Never-Never Land

The story of Peter Pan and Never-Never Land was written by J. M. Barrie. In Barrie's novel there are only two ways to get to Never-Never Land: children who are at the edge of sleep can sometimes travel there, or Peter Pan may take them there. Female visitors are not allowed, except for Wendy Darling, whom Peter Pan takes there to be mother to the Lost Boys. Never-Never Land is inhabited by fairies, mermaids, pirates, Red Indians, lost boys, and of course, Peter Pan.

Oz

The large country of Oz is divided into four sections. In each region the people wear different colors. In Munchkin Land they wear blue. In Winkie Country they wear yellow. In Quadling Country, it is red, and in Gillikin, it is purple. The country is completely surrounded by desert, and its capital is the Emerald City. The stories about Oz, including *The Wonderful Wizard of Oz*, were written by L. Frank Baum in the early 1900s.

Pal-uL-Don

Pal-uL-Don is the jungle home of Tarzan. It is located somewhere in Zaire, near the west coast of Africa, just south of the equator. In the novel by Edgar Rice Burroughs, Tarzan and his parents are shipwrecked here, and shortly after, his parents both die. Tarzan is then raised by an ape.

Pleasure Island

In the book *Pinocchio* by C. Collodi, Pleasure Island is a country where there are no books, no teachers, and no learning, only fun and amusement. Boys are lured there to play, but once they arrive, they are turned into donkeys and put to hard labor. Pinocchio finds this out the hard way. In the original version of *Pinocchio*, Pleasure Island is known as Cocagne, or the Land of the Boobies.

Shangri-la

Shangri-la is described in *Lost Horizon*, a novel by James Hilton. It is located in a valley in Tibet, on the "rooftop of the world." A Buddhist monastery sits on a mountain overlooking the valley, and the lamas (Buddhist monks) rule

over Shangri-la. Shangri-la can only be reached by foot. There is no crime there, and it is a place free from worldly troubles. Life spans there are very long so the inhabitants age very, very slowly. However, once one leaves Shangri-la, the signs of aging show themselves in an extreme way.

Sleepy Hollow

The Legend of Sleepy Hollow was written by Washington Irving. Sleepy Hollow is a dreamy village set high in the hills above the Hudson River. It's filled with superstitious people who live in a constant dreamlike state. Sleepy Hollow is the home of the ill-fated schoolteacher Ichabod Crane, the headless horseman, and other ghosts.

Treasure Island

Robert Louis Stevenson's *Treasure Island* was published in 1882. In the book he describes an island off the coast of Mexico covered with woods and swamps. The deserted island holds a valuable treasure buried by Captain Flint, a buccaneer who killed those who witnessed the burial. Long John Silver, Bill Bones, and Ben Gunn are some of the characters who pursue the treasure buried on Treasure Island.

Wonderland

Wonderland is located somewhere near Oxford, England, on the bank of the Thames River. One must pass through a rabbit hole to enter Wonderland. Once through the hole, there is a long fall downward to the underground halls and passageways of Wonderland. Any food or drink consumed there makes one shrink or grow to fit through the doors. Among the inhabitants are: a pack of cards, including the famous Queen of Hearts, a white rabbit, a mad hatter, a Cheshire cat, and a caterpillar. One can follow Alice's travels there by reading *Alice's Adventures in Wonderland*, by Lewis Carroll.

Xanadu

Xanadu is described by Samuel Taylor Coleridge in his poem "Kubla Khan." In Coleridge's poem, the exotic emperor Kubla Khan orders his pleasure dome to be built in the kingdom of Xanadu. The magnificent palace covers ten miles of land. Ancient enchanted forests, caves of ice, and the sacred river Alph can be found in the kingdom.

LOST CITIES

• •

The five cities included here were all uncovered after years of being deserted and in ruins. The excavation of these cities has taught us much about the way of life of people who lived thousands of years ago.

Angkor

Angkor was an ancient city in Cambodia. It was the capital of the Khmer Empire, which disintegrated toward the end of the thirteenth century. A little over one hundred years ago, it was discovered by French archaeologists, deep in the jungles of Cambodia. The gates and walls of Angkor were covered with jungle growth. When the growth was cleared away, thousands of carvings depicting life in the Khmer Empire were found. The site covered forty square miles and included several capitols of the ruined empire. There were extensive canals, which were used to irrigate rice fields, and pools dotted the city. The discovery of Angkor revealed the magnificent architecture, sculpture, and technology of the Asian jungle people, the Khmers.

Babylon

There are many songs and stories about Babylon, an ancient city famed for being a place of luxury and of sensual living. This enormous city was the capital of Babylonia in ancient Mesopotamia, now called Iraq. Babylon flourished for twelve hundred years, from 1750 B.C. on. It was situated on a wide open plain and surrounded by a large moat. In the center of the city was the palace of the king. The Hanging Gardens of Babylon, one of the seven wonders of the ancient world, were built on the palace grounds. Babylon was also said to be the site of the famed "Tower of Babel." The city was captured by the Persians and eventually deserted. Today it is a desolate ruin surrounded by scrubby fields.

Machu Picchu

Machu Picchu is located high in the Andes Mountains of Peru, straddled between two mountain peaks. It was the fortress city of the ancient Incas. When this city was found by archaeologists early in the twentieth century, it was virtually intact. The city was built of stone, and the buildings were linked by steps, not streets, all set on terraces along the mountainside. More than 3,000 steps were built on the site. When the Spanish arrived in South America in the sixteenth century, they conquered the Incan empire, but it is believed they never found Machu Picchu. The extensive ruins of this great city can still be viewed today.

Mycenae

This Greek city was once the major center of life around the Mediterranean Sea. Mycenae flourished from 1900 B.C. to 900 B.C., and it was once the home of the Greek king Agamemnon. When the city was uncovered in the late 1800s, archaeologists found golden masks, which were buried with kings. The city was surrounded by a wall made of such huge stones it is still a wonder as to how the wall was built. Inside the wall archaeologists found palaces and homes with carvings depicting life in ancient Greece.

Pompeii

Pompeii was once a port city and resort for wealthy Romans. It was damaged by an earthquake in A.D. 63 and buried by a volcanic eruption sixteen years later. The ruins of the city were preserved by the layers of ash and cinder. When the city was uncovered in the 1700s, walls, temples, baths, theaters, money, jewelry, food, and even skeletons were found. The ruins of this ancient city can be viewed today. Pompeii is near Naples, Italy.

NEW NAMES FOR OLD PLACES

· ·

Because the world is constantly changing, it might seem as if some places on this earth have disappeared. But when new leaders or a new people take over, they sometimes choose different names to signify hope and change. Here are the new and old names for some places in the world.

· · · · · · · · · · · · · ·

Now	Then

Middle East

Israel	Palestine
Iran	Persia
Iraq	Mesopotamia

South Pacific — **Oceania**

Fiji Islands	Cannibal Islands
Tonga	Friendly Islands
Rarotonga	Goodenough Islands

Asia

Sri Lanka	Ceylon
Taiwan	Formosa
Thailand	Siam
Vietnam-Cambodia-Laos	French Indochina

Americas

Belize	British Honduras
Guyana	British Guiana
Haiti & Dominican Republic	Hispaniola

Africa

Chad	French Equatorial Africa
Congo	French Equatorial Africa
Ethiopia	Abyssinia
Gabon	French Equatorial Africa
Ghana	Gold Coast
Kenya	British East Africa
Lesotho	Basutoland
Zaire	Belgian Congo
Zambia	Northern Rhodesia
Zimbabwe	Southern Rhodesia

PLACES TO BE
(Figuratively Speaking)
• •

There is no real cloud nine, of course, but it has come to be associated with a happy place to be. The expressions that follow describe various states of mind and conditions that people experience. How many of these places have you visited?

Behind the Eight Ball. To be in a dangerous position from which it is impossible to escape. The phrase comes from the game of pool.

Beyond the Pale. Outside an area's bounds and the protection and privileges of that territory.

Cloud Nine. To be high up and euphoric in spirit. The Weather Bureau divides clouds into types. The highest type is nine.

Davy Jones's Locker. An old sailors' term for the oceans' depths and death for the sailor who went there.

Ivory Tower. Where intellectuals go to get away from the world and think.

The Land of Milk and Honey. A place rich in resources. The phrase is from the Old Testament. Also called the Promised Land.

The Land of Nod. The world of sleep.

No Man's Land is a piece of wasteland. In fourteenth-century London it was an execution site for criminals who were beheaded. Their bodies were left to rot there and as a result no one wanted to own this land.

Podunk. A remote, small, isolated town.

The School of Hard Knocks. Learning through life experiences rather than through formal education in a school.

Seventh Heaven. A state of bliss. It is from the ancient theory of astronomy that there were seven rings of stars and the seventh was the highest.

The Twilight Zone. An ill-defined area between fantasy and reality.

SECTION III:

THINGS TO KNOW

The things included here are as diverse as clothing, rocks, walls, and quests. You'll read about a dictator's wife who owned three thousand pairs of shoes, and a wall that separated a city and its people for decades until it suddenly came tumbling down. And, you'll learn that some quests, such as those featured in the Indiana Jones movies, are centuries old.

AGES

• •

Ages are periods of time in history. They mark human progress, signify a way of thinking, or reflect the influence of a people. Listed below in time sequence are nine ages to know.

Ice Age

When people say something is "as old as the Ice Age," they are talking about a time that began 2.3 million years ago. Ice Ages (there were several) were periods in the earth's history when sheets of ice covered large portions of land. The most recent ice age ended 10,000 years ago.

Stone Age

The longest period in human history, the Stone Age began some two million years ago and marked the emergence of Homo sapiens (man), who used stone implements and weapons.

Bronze Age

The Bronze Age lasted from 3,000 B.C. to 1,000 B.C., and was considered the first technological age. People used metals to make tools and weapons.

Iron Age

A period of time marked by the general use of iron for tools, vehicles, money, weapons, and objects of art. The Iron Age followed the Bronze Age (1,000 B.C.) and extended to modern times.

Classical Age

This period of time, from 500 B.C. to A.D. 500, marked the dominance of the Greek and Roman cultures. It was the heyday of the art, literature, architecture, and philosophy of the Greeks and Romans.

Middle Ages

The Middle Ages extended from the fall of the Roman Empire in A.D. 476 to 1500. The Middle Ages separate the ancient history of civilization from the modern history. The Middle Ages are also called *medieval* times or, by some, the Dark Ages.

Age of Reason

Also known as the Enlightenment, the Age of Reason characterizes seventeenth- and eighteenth-century England and France. Intellectuals of this time believed science and reason were the basis for all knowledge.

Victorian Age

A period in English history, marked by the reign of Queen Victoria, 1837–1901. A time of great literature and booming industry, this age has also been labeled one of prudish thinking.

Jazz Age

A wild period in American cultural history from the end of World War I (1918) to the fall of the stock market (1929). Dancing and drinking to the sounds of great jazz band music marked this time.

Space Age

When the Soviet Union launched the *Sputnik* in 1957, the Space Age began. That date was followed by further space exploration, including missions to the moon, space travel, and unmanned planet probes, which are ongoing.

CLOTHING: FROM HEAD TO TOE

here is an old saying that goes: "It's the clothes that make the man." So we often remember people because of the unusual items of clothing they wear. Beginning in biblical times, and moving right on to figures from books and movies and contemporary rock stars, people have been identified by significant pieces of clothing. Would Dorothy ever have gotten home without her ruby red slippers?

Biblical Attire

Adam and Eve's Fig-Leaf Aprons

When Adam and Eve were sent out of the Garden of Eden for their sin, they realized they were naked and covered themselves with aprons made of fig leaves. Their story is told in the Book of Genesis.

Haman's Three-Cornered Hat

According to the Bible, Haman was a cruel king who wanted to kill all the Jews in his kingdom. He always wore a three-cornered hat. Purim is a Jewish holiday that commemorates the Jewish victory over Haman. *Hamantaschen*,

cookies shaped like Haman's three-cornered hat, are served on Purim.

Joseph's Coat of Many Colors

In the Old Testament, Joseph was the favorite son of Jacob. When he was seventeen years old, his father gave him an elegant, long-sleeved, many-colored coat. The colors of the coat were said to be yellow, wine, red, and dark green. The gift of this coat showed his preference for Joseph, which angered his brothers.

Samson's Long Hair

Samson, a popular hero in the Old Testament, was famed for his great strength. At his birth, his mother vowed she would never cut his hair so that he would remain strong. Later Samson fell in love with Delilah. She betrayed him by cutting his hair while he slept, and his strength was lost.

Solomon's Ring

King Solomon was said to have a ring with a magic mirror that gave him the answers to difficult questions. This is one explanation for his uncanny gift of wisdom.

Celebrities' Dress

Johnny Cash's Black Outfit

When Johnny Cash first performed in a church in North Memphis, Tennessee, he wanted the band members to dress alike. The three musicians all had black shirts so they wore them. From that day on Johnny Cash has always performed in black.

Charlie Chaplin's Derby

Charlie Chaplin was one of the cinema's first major stars. In his best-known role as the Little Tramp, Chaplin wears his baggy suit and famous derby. Chaplin later said of the Little Tramp, "The moment I was dressed *he* was born."

Isadora Duncan's Scarf

Isadora Duncan was a famous American dancer who lived from 1878 to 1927. She was well known as a teacher of free-form dance. Her long scarf became famous when it caused her death. One day while taking off in an open-roofed car, Isadora Duncan's scarf caught in the wheel and choked her to death.

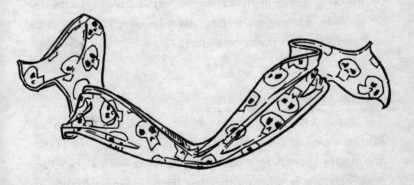

• • • • • • • • • • • • • •

Peter Falk's Raincoat

Peter Falk plays the role of a Los Angeles detective in the TV series *Columbo*. He is always seen wearing a stained brown raincoat over an old suit and worn shoes. His appearance and manner make him seem inept, but he always catches the murderer.

Madonna's Lingerie

Madonna, born Louise Veronica Ciccone, became a rock superstar in the 1980s. She became famous for wearing her bras as outerwear while performing.

Roy Orbison's Sunglasses

Roy Orbison, a great rock and roll singer, always appeared on stage in sunglasses. This trademark came about by mistake. Early in his career he forgot his eyeglasses on an airplane. Having only sunglasses, he wore them onstage and performed in them ever after.

Minnie Pearl's Hat

Sarah Ophelia Colley Cannon, otherwise known as Minnie Pearl, is a TV personality who starred on *Hee Haw*. She always appears in a wide-brimmed hat with a price tag hanging from it. She and her hat have become a fixture in American folk humor.

Tina Turner's Wigs

Tina Turner has been a well-known rock and roll performer since the 1970s. She appears on stage or TV wearing a tight miniskirt, high heels, and often wearing a wild-looking wig.

Stevie Wonder's Cornrows

Stevie Wonder, one of the finest soul singers and songwriters, wears his long black hair in cornrows and draped in beads. He became a star with his first record in 1963, when he was only thirteen years old.

Clothes in History

Johnny Appleseed's Frying-Pan Hat

John Chapman was an American folk hero known as Johnny Appleseed. He wore a frying pan on his head as he traveled around the country planting apple seeds in the early 1800s.

Yasir Arafat's Headdress

Yasir Arafat is an Arab leader of the Palestine Liberation Organization. He always appears in public in the same outfit: a checkered head scarf with a peaked top and tasseled tail called a *kaffiyeh*. He also wears a military shirt and trousers in matching olive green with a belt, boots, Rolex watch, and revolver.

Beau Brummell's Ascot

Beau Brummell was an Englishman who lived from 1778–1840 and was known for his exquisite dress. He spent hours in front of the mirror making the folds in his white linen neckcloth just right and the knot no less than perfect. He started the style of ascots (a broad neckcloth) for men.

Buffalo Bill's Leather Fringed Jacket

William Frederick Cody took the name Buffalo Bill and made a living as a frontier showman. He took his "Wild West" show around the U.S. in the late 1800s. He created the "western look" with his leather fringed jacket, large military boots, and big belt.

Barbara Bush's Pearls

Barbara Bush, wife of U.S. President George Bush, put her fashion signature on pearls. She wears her costume pearl collar wherever she goes, whether it's to homeless shelters or inaugural balls.

Davy Crockett's Coonskin Hat

Davy Crockett was an American frontiersman who became a folk hero and legend. His trademark was his coonskin hat, which had a fur tail hanging down the back.

Ben Franklin's Bifocals

Ben Franklin, an American statesman and inventor, is always pictured wearing glasses. He created bifocals because he needed one kind of lens for reading and another kind for other activities. Rather than carry two sets of eyeglasses, he had two lenses put into one pair of glasses.

Lady Godiva's Long Hair

According to legend, Lady Godiva was an Englishwoman who lived during the eleventh century. To protest the heavy taxes imposed on the people of her town, she rode naked on horseback through the streets of Coventry. Her long hair covered her.

King Henry VIII's Rings

King Henry the VIII of England was reported to have kept a large stock of rings on hand just in case he wanted to remarry. He had a total of six wives. In 1530 his personal inventory listed 234 women's rings.

Jackie Kennedy's Pillbox Hat

Jacqueline Kennedy Onassis was the wife of President John F. Kennedy, the thirty-fifth president of the United States. During the Kennedy administration she popularized the wearing of the small oval hat with straight sides and a flat top, known as the pillbox.

Imelda Marcos's Shoes

President Ferdinand Marcos of the Philippines and his wife, Imelda, were forced to leave the Philippines in 1986, when it was discovered they had stolen billions of dollars from the Philippine people. After their hurried departure, it was revealed that Imelda owned 3,000 pairs of shoes, which were left in the palace.

Mark Twain's White Suit

Mark Twain was the pen name of Samuel Langhorne Clemens, who lived from 1835 to 1910. He is known as one of the best and most popular American authors. He often appeared in public dressed in a three-piece white linen suit.

Clothes in Story

Alice in Wonderland's Headband

In the illustrations for *Alice's Adventures Through the Looking Glass*, Lewis Carroll's 1865 book, Alice is shown wearing a headband to hold her hair in place. This began a style that's been popular with girls ever since.

Cinderella's Glass Slippers

In Charles Perrault's version of the fairy tale, the glass slipper worn by Cinderella is lost when she hurries home after the ball. The prince who finds the slipper conducts a door-to-door search for the woman whose foot fits the glass slipper and finally finds Cinderella.

Dorothy's Ruby Red Slippers

Dorothy, in *The Wonderful Wizard of Oz*, written by L. Frank Baum, is given sparkling shoes by the good witch. These shoes protect her from the wicked witch and help her get back to Kansas. In the movie version the shoes are sparkling ruby red.

The Emperor's
New ✦ Clothes

The Emperor's New Clothes

"The Emperor's New Clothes" is a funny fairy tale by Hans Christian Andersen. The Emperor is a vain man who is fooled into believing two tailors will create the most elegant robe ever made for him. The Emperor gives them gold for precious cloth. They keep the gold and make an invisible robe that they say only the wise can see. The vain Emperor parades through the streets in his new "robe" and is laughed at by all because he is really naked.

Hester Prynne's Embroidered Scarlet Letter

The scarlet letter worn by Hester in Nathaniel Hawthorne's novel *The Scarlet Letter* is meant to serve as a warning that Hester was a sinner. Hester is made to wear a red "A" because she committed adultery, breaking the laws of society of that time.

Little Lord Fauntleroy's Black Velvet Suit

Little Lord Fauntleroy is the hero in Frances Hodgson Burnett's 1886 novel of the same name. He is a seven-year-old with long, curly golden hair, who wears a velvet knickerbocker suit. This black velvet suit consists of a jacket and knickers, which became a popular dress of the period.

Little Red Riding Hood's Cloak

Charles Perrault, a French fairy tale writer, wrote *Little Red Riding Hood*. In the story, Little Red Riding Hood's grandmother gives her the red cape, which in turn gives the girl her name.

Pippi Longstocking's Mismatched Stockings

Pippi is the daring nine-year-old heroine of Astrid Lindgren's books. She lives alone most of the time, taking care of her own needs. Her trademark is the long, unmatched socks she wears. This is because she has trouble finding two socks that are the same.

Sherlock Holmes's Hat

Sherlock Holmes was created by Arthur Conan Doyle as the ultimate detective. His checkered deerstalker hat has become a classic and serves as a remembrance of what upper-class Englishmen of the late nineteenth century wore.

Tarzan's Loincloth

Tarzan is a character in a series of novels by Edgar Rice Burroughs. Growing up with apes in the African jungle, Tarzan has only a loincloth to wear. He continues to wear his loincloth throughout his life.

DOCUMENTS

• •

Throughout history, documents have caused revolutions, and they have created more just societies. Many important documents, such as the Declaration of Independence, were written hundreds of years ago, and are still the basis for laws today. In some cases, we even have the original document, but most have been destroyed over the years and we know them only because they have been passed on in other forms.

Code of Hammurabi

Hammurabi was a king of ancient Babylonia. He is remembered for the code of laws he wrote and set in stone. Among the laws was, "If a man put out the eye of another man, his eye shall be put out." The code of Hammurabi dates back to the eighteenth century B.C. and is considered one of the greatest of the ancient codes.

Hippocratic Oath

Hippocrates the Great was a Greek physician who lived from 460–370 BC. His medical beliefs are represented in the Hippocratic Oath. Under this oath (which is still taken today), doctors promise to help the sick and not to injure them in any way. Hippocrates is known as the "father of medicine," because he was among the first to replace superstition with science in the treatment of illness.

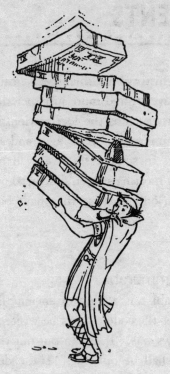

Magna Charta

Magna Charta is Latin for "great charter." In England, in 1215, King John reluctantly signed this document. It limited the power of kings and outlined human rights for their subjects. Most important in the Magna Charta is the claim that individuals may not be jailed or punished without a trial by jury. There are four copies of this document in existence today.

Mayflower Compact

Before the Pilgrims disembarked from their ship, the

Mayflower, they drew up and signed an agreement of self-government by the will of the majority. The year was 1620 and the document, signed by 41 male adults, became the first such agreement to be enforced in America. The original document was lost, but a version of it was recorded in *The History of Plymouth Plantation*, written by William Bradford, a governor of Plymouth Colony.

Declaration of Independence

One of the greatest political documents of all time was written primarily by Thomas Jefferson. It announced the separation of the thirteen colonies from Great Britain and created the country of the United States of America. The Declaration of Independence was signed on July 4, 1776, marking the birth of a nation. The government of this new nation was based on what the declaration called the citizens' natural rights: life, liberty, and the pursuit of happiness.

Communist Manifesto

In 1848, two Germans, Karl Marx and Friedrich Engels, wrote and distributed a pamphlet called "The Communist Manifesto." It stated that as a result of class struggle, privately owned businesses would eventually be overthrown and replaced with communism. Communism is a theory that supports the idea of ownership of goods in common instead of in private. The doctrine of "The Communist Manifesto" is known as Marxism and is the basis for modern Communist principles.

QUESTS

• •

A quest involves seeking something. Those who embark upon a quest usually have many adventures and face dangers of every sort. Here are four famous quests.

Ark of the Covenant

In the movie *Raiders of the Lost Ark*, Indiana Jones, an adventurer and archaeologist, sets out to find the Ark. The Ark is believed to have the tablets containing the Ten Commandments handed down from God to Moses. The Ark is valuable and said to have mystical powers. Anyone who possesses it will be invincible. In the movie, Indiana Jones battles the armies of Hitler to capture the Ark. After many adventures, he finds the Ark, recaptures it from the Germans, and hands it over to the U.S. Army.

Fountain of Youth

The Fountain of Youth was said to contain the water of life, which had been in the Garden of Eden. It was thought to be located in the Far East. When the fifteenth-century Spanish explorers explored America, they thought they were in the Far East. Ponce de León, a Spanish explorer, heard the legend of the Fountain of Youth. In his search for it he found Florida. There he drank from every spring he could find, hoping that the waters would make him live forever. He did not find a fountain of youth and died in 1521.

Golden Fleece

According to Greek mythology, there was a sheep whose wool was made of gold. When the sheep died, its fleece was removed and hidden. Jason, a Greek hero, goes in search of the golden fleece. Jason and his men, called the Argonauts, battle dragons and outsmart kings to find the Golden Fleece. They succeed and return home with it.

Holy Grail

The Grail is said to be the chalice used at the Last Supper of Jesus Christ. The legend of King Arthur tells how his knights go in search of the Holy Grail. Each begins his search alone in the dark forest. Sir Galahad, a knight of exceptional virtue, finds the Grail. He is the only knight able to see the Grail in all its shining splendor. After he finds and sees the Grail, Galahad disappears.

ROCKS AND WALLS

There are rocks and walls in this world that have a sense of lasting mystery. We may not know the origin of the mystery, but people still believe in their magical or special powers. Some walls have also been built to divide countries, and they represent political power.

Rocks

Blarney Stone

It's been said that those who kiss the Blarney Stone will be given the gift of persuasive eloquence, also known as "blarney." The Blarney Stone is located at the top of Blarney Castle, near Cork, Ireland. To kiss the Blarney Stone one must lean backward with one's head down between the castle wall and the parapet. There are iron bars there to hold on to for support.

Plymouth Rock

In 1620 the Pilgrims landed in America and supposedly set foot on Plymouth Rock. This rock is a large granite boulder located in Plymouth, Massachusetts. Over the years, it has been moved several times and pieces of it have been sold as souvenirs. Today it is enshrined under a canopy near

Plymouth Village, where it serves as a memorial to the Pilgrim landing.

"The Rock"

Alcatraz Island, located in San Francisco Bay in California, is known as "the rock." The U.S. Army used the twelve-acre island from 1859 to 1934, when it became a federal prison and was called "the rock." As a prison, "the rock" was considered escape-proof. The prison closed in 1963. Today the island is part of the National Park Service.

Rock of Gibraltar

Gibraltar is a peninsula connected to Spain. Most of the peninsula, which stretches into the Mediterranean Sea, is a rock ridge known as the Rock of Gibraltar (sometimes called the "rock," too). Composed of gray limestone and shale, it is dotted with caves and tunnels. In ancient times the Rock of Gibraltar marked the limits of the known world.

Rosetta Stone

Only four feet by two feet, this slab of basalt is so valuable it has been named and placed in a museum. The Rosetta Stone is an ancient Egyptian monument inscribed with hieroglyphic writing. Because it had the same text in two languages and three alphabets, it provided a key to scholars to decipher ancient Egyptian writing. The Rosetta Stone was found by Napoleon's troops near Rosetta, Egypt. Today it is in the British Museum in London.

Stonehenge

Stonehenge is a grouping of large stones near Salisbury, England. These large stones were laid out during the Stone Age in a formation thought to be used as a temple and/or for astronomical observations. Historians believe Stonehenge was built over a five-hundred-year period (2000–1500 B.C.).

Walls

Berlin Wall

This wall once extended twenty-nine miles through Berlin, and separated East Berlin from West Berlin. The East Germans built the wall in 1961 to keep East Germans from fleeing to West Germany. It was nicknamed "The Wall of Shame" by those who fled before it was built. The city is again one Berlin and the capital of a united Germany. In

November of 1989, the gates of the Wall were opened to allow East Germans to pass into West Germany.

Great Wall of China

This 1,500-mile-long wall was once a line of defense for Imperial China. It is the longest fortification ever built. In the third century B.C., the Chinese emperor connected and extended walls that had been built by feudal lords. From 1368 to 1644, during the Ming dynasty, most of the wall was completed. It was built mostly of rubble and averages twenty-five feet in height. The Great Wall extends across northern China to the Yellow Sea.

Hadrian's Wall

In A.D. 122, Hadrian, the Roman emperor, ordered this wall built to protect Roman Britain from invaders. The wall extends 73½ miles across Britain from Wallsend to

Bowness. At some points the wall was twenty feet thick at the base and twelve feet high. Now only scattered fragments of the wall remain.

The Vietnam Veterans' Memorial

The Wall, as it is commonly known, is located in Washington, D.C. It is considered America's "wailing wall" and was designed in 1981 by twenty-one-year-old Maya Ying Lin, an architecture student at Yale University.

Wailing Wall

This fifty-nine-foot-high wall is located in Jerusalem. Parts of the wall once surrounded the ancient Temple of Solomon. Beginning in the Middle Ages, Jews gathered at the foot of the wall to bewail the destruction of the temple. For many the wall has been a symbol of Judaism. Since 1948, Jerusalem has been divided into the Old City held by Jordan and the new city held by Israel.

A CALENDAR OF SPORTS EVENTS

Each year sports fans look forward to the season of their favorite sporting game. Even if you're not a fan, sometimes it's helpful to know when certain events take place. A listing of major yearly sporting events follows.

A Calendar of Worldwide Sporting Events

Month	Event	Sport
January	Super Bowl	Professional Football
	Post-Season College Bowls: Rose Cotton Orange Hula	
	Pro Bowl	All-Star Football Bowl
February	Millrose Games	Track and Field
	Daytona 500	Auto Racing

Month	Event	Sport
March	Iditarod	Sled Dog Racing
	NCAA Playoffs Begin	College Basketball
	National College Bowling Championships	
April	Masters Tournament	Golf
	Stanley Cup Playoffs	Hockey
	Boston Marathon	Running
May	Indianapolis 500	Auto Racing
	Kentucky Derby Preakness Stakes Belmont Stakes	Horse Racing (Triple Crown)
	Monte Carlo Grand Prix	Auto Racing
	NBA Playoffs (finals)	Basketball

Month	Event	Sport
June	Wimbledon	Tennis
	College World Series	Baseball
July	Major League All-Star Game	Baseball
	Calgary Stampede	Rodeo
	Tour de France	Bicycle Race

Month	Event	Sport
August	PGA Championship	Golf
	Little League World Series	Baseball
September	U.S. Open	Tennis
October	World Series	Baseball
	Ironman/Woman Triathlon	(2.4 mile swim, 112 mile bicycle race and marathon)
	Daytona Pro/Am	Motorcycle
November	New York City Marathon	Running
November/ December	Triple Crown	Surfing (1-month event)
December	NFL Playoffs Begin	Football

THINGS NAMED AFTER PEOPLE

• •

Most of us don't think about the origin of the names of everyday household objects. Some of the things listed below are named for the famous people who invented them.

Amp. An amp or ampere, is a unit of electric current. André-Marie Ampère was a nineteenth-century French physicist. In 1883 the ampere was named in his honor.

Baedeker. A Baedeker (BAYD-i-kər) is any kind of guidebook. Early in the 1800s, Karl Baedeker, a German printer, began publishing travel guides that listed places to eat and stay.

Cardigan. The popular sweater that buttons down the front was named not for its creator but for the man who popularized it. He was an Englishman, James Brudenell, the seventh Earl of Cardigan, who lived in the mid-1800s.

Celsius. Anders Celsius (SEL-see-əs) was an astronomer who lived in Sweden in the early 1700s. He devised the centi-

grade thermometer, which measures temperatures from freezing to boiling on a scale of 0° to 100° Celsius.

Fahrenheit. Gabriel Fahrenheit was an eighteenth-century German. He devised a thermometer that measures temperature. On the Fahrenheit scale, 32° above zero is freezing, 212° above zero is boiling.

Ferris Wheel.

In 1893 an American inventor, George Washington Gale Ferris, displayed his gigantic revolving wheel at the Chicago World's Fair. It was named the Ferris wheel after its creator.

Franklin Stove.

This is a heating stove that resembles an open fireplace. Benjamin Franklin, the prolific American inventor and statesman, invented it. It is the only one of his many inventions named after him.

Geiger Counter.

Early in the twentieth century, Hans Geiger, a German physicist, devised the first instrument to detect and measure radioactivity. It is the Geiger counter.

Macadam.

This commonly used road pavement is made of small compacted stones bound with tar or asphalt. Macadam was developed by John McAdam, a Scottish engineer, in 1824.

Mach.

Unusually high air speeds are measured in Mach numbers, such as Mach 1, Mach 2. The Mach numbers are the number of times the speed of sound. The name is from Ernst Mach, an Austrian physicist who studied objects moving at the speed of sound.

Molotov Cocktail. This weapon consists of a bottle filled with gasoline or any flammable liquid. It explodes after it is ignited and thrown. The Finns used these bombs against the Soviets in 1939. They named the bomb after Molotov, who was the Soviet minister of foreign affairs.

Ohm. An ohm is a unit of resistance in electricity. It was named after Georg Ohm (1787–1854), a German physicist, for his work in electricity.

Pasteurization. The process of pasteurizing kills harmful food bacteria by gentle heating. Louis Pasteur, a French chemist, devised the process in the nineteenth century.

Pompadour. This is a hairstyle in which the hair is combed into a high mound at the front of the head. It was created by Madame de Pompadour, a famous eighteenth-century Frenchwoman.

Pullman. A railroad sleeping car is simply known as a Pullman. George Pullman, an American manufacturer, built the first railroad sleeping car, which went into service in 1865.

Sandwich. John Montague, the fourth Earl of Sandwich, was an eighteenth-century English diplomat. He was an around-the-clock gambler. He wouldn't stop gambling to sit down to dinner, so his servant brought him meat between two pieces of bread. This creation was soon called a sandwich.

Shrapnel. Fragments that are scattered by explosives are called shrapnel. Henry Shrapnel was a nineteenth-century British artillery officer who invented explosives that encased lead balls and gunpowder in a shell.

Van Allen Belt. The layers of electrically charged particles above Earth's atmosphere are known as the Van Allen Belt.

James Van Allen, a twentieth-century American physicist, discovered this belt.

Zeppelin. Count Ferdinand von Zeppelin was a German
military officer. In 1900 he invented the rigid airship known
as a zeppelin.

. . . .

SECTION IV:

SOME WORDS AND NUMBERS TO KNOW

In this section you will find some words and numbers that often come up in conversations, and appear in books and newspapers. You will find fancy foreign phrases and colorful lingo that's used to order food in diners. Also included are abbreviations, "word people" (whose names have become adjectives), and ten important years from our history.

ABBREVIATIONS

● ●

The abbreviations listed below are used commonly in our culture. In fact, they're used so often, it's sometimes hard to remember the full words they stand for. How often have you read about the "GOP" in the newspaper? You probably know it means the Republican party, but do you know what the letters stand for?

AC	air conditioning
A.D.	anno domini (the year of our Lord)
A.M.	ante meridien (morning, before noon)
APB	all points bulletin
ASAP	as soon as possible
B and B	bed and breakfast
B.C.	before Christ
BYO	bring your own
CIA	Central Intelligence Agency
COD	cash on delivery
DA	district attorney
d/b/a	doing business as
DC	direct current
DJ	disc jockey
DOA	dead on arrival
DOB	date of birth
EPA	Environmental Protection Agency
ERA	Equal Rights Amendment, or, in baseball, earned run average

ESP	extrasensory perception
FBI	Federal Bureau of Investigation
FDA	Food and Drug Administration
GOP	Grand Old Party (Republican party)
HM	Her Majesty or His Majesty
HQ	headquarters
ID	identification
IRS	Internal Revenue Service
ISBN	International Standard Book Number
KGB	Russian for the Soviet secret police and intelligence agency
KKK	Ku Klux Klan
MIA	missing in action
mpg	miles per gallon
mph	miles per hour

NAACP	National Association for the Advancement of Colored People
NASA	National Aeronautics and Space Administration
NOW	National Organization for Women
P.M.	post meridien (afternoon)
POW	prisoner of war
PPS	additional postscript
PS	postscript
qt	quiet, in secret ("on the qt")
RDA	recommended daily allowance
RIP	rest in peace

RSVP	French initials for "please reply"
SASE	self-addressed stamped envelope
SPCA	Society for the Prevention of Cruelty to Animals
SWAT	Special Weapons and Tactics
TNT	trinitrotoluene (an explosive)
vs	versus (against)
YA	young adult

Catchphrases

Although millions of people may use a catchphrase, its

author isn't always known. Popular catchphrases have been used to lead marches and political movements. They are used in songs and written on posters. The catchphrases below symbolize the era in which they were written.

Kilroy was here. World War II soldiers' graffiti scrawled on walls everywhere in Europe in the 1940s.

Better dead than red. Anti-Communist phrase of the Cold War.

That's the way the cookie crumbles. Saying of the 1950s.

Don't trust anyone over 30. Counterculture phrase of the 1960s.

See you later, alligator. . . . In a while, crocodile. First said by Bill Haley, a rock and roll singer of the late 1950s and early 1960s.

America, love it or leave it. Slogan during the Vietnam War era of the late 1960s.

Everyone will be world famous for fifteen minutes. Said by pop artist Andy Warhol in 1968; frequently quoted in the late 1980s after Warhol's death.

Power to the people. Originally a black power slogan and then taken up by the radical student movement of the 1960s and 1970s.

Keep on truckin'. Originally a slogan of a cartoon character created by cartoonist Robert Crumb. It was popularized by the music group the Grateful Dead in the 1970s.

Today is the first day of the rest of your life. A wall slogan from the 1970s.

Go for it. A rallying cry for success in the 1980s.

A kinder, gentler nation. Frequently used by George Bush in his campaign for the presidency, 1988.

Don't worry, be happy. Song lyrics by Bobby McFerrin that became popular in 1989.

DATES

· ·

The days and years to remember listed below mark important historic events. Remembering these dates will help give you a sense of the history of Western civilization.

Nine Days to Remember

Ides of March   March 15. On this day in 44 B.C., Julius Caesar, emperor of Rome, was assassinated.

Independence Day   July 4, 1776. On this day the Declaration of Independence was signed in the U.S.

Black Tuesday   October 29, 1929. On this day the stock market fell and the Great Depression began in the U.S.

Pearl Harbor Day December 7, 1941. On this day the Japanese attacked the U.S. fleet at Pearl Harbor in Hawaii, and the U.S. entered World War II. Also known as "a date that will live in infamy," as described by then U.S. President Franklin Delano Roosevelt.

D Day June 6, 1944. The Allied troops landed on the Normandy beaches in France. It was the beginning of the end for the Germans in World War II.

V-E Day May 8, 1945. The Germans surrendered and World War II ended in Europe.

Hiroshima Day August 6, 1945. The first atomic bomb was dropped by the Americans on Hiroshima, Japan. The Japanese surrendered on September 2, ending World War II.

Rosa Parks Day	December 1, 1955. In Montgomery, Alabama, Rosa Parks, a black woman, is arrested for refusing to give up her seat to a white person on a public bus. Her action marks the beginning of the civil rights struggle in America.
Presidential Resignation Day	August 9, 1974. President Richard Nixon is the only U.S. president to resign his office. His resignation was the result of the "Watergate" scandal.

Ten Years to Remember

1066	The Battle of Hastings marks the conquest of England by the Normans. William the Conqueror becomes king of England.
1215	The Magna Charta is signed by King John at Runnymede, England. It guarantees rights of the common man by limiting the power of the king.
1492	Christopher Columbus, sailing under the flag of Spain, crosses the Atlantic and lands in America.
1588	The Spanish Armada sails against England but is defeated by the English. This victory opens the world to colonization and trade by the English.

1607	The first permanent European settlement is founded in America at Jamestown, Virginia.
1620	The Pilgrims land in Plymouth, Massachusetts, and found a colony.
1776	The Declaration of Independence is signed, marking the birth of a new nation, the United States of America.
1861–1865	The War between the States, or the Civil War, rages in America. The Union defeats the Confederates and the country stays united.
1914–1918	The "Great War" or World War I, takes place in Europe. The *Allies* (France, Britain, Russia, and the U.S.) fought the *Central Powers* (Germany, Austria-Hungary, and Turkey).
1939–1945	World War II takes place in Europe and the South Pacific. The *Allies* (Britain, U.S., and the Soviet Union) battle the *Axis* (Germany, Italy, and Japan). The Axis are defeated by the Allies.

FAMILIAR FOREIGN PHRASES

You don't have to speak French or understand Latin to know some foreign phrases. Many of these phrases may already be in your vocabulary. If not, now you can get to know these familiar foreign expressions.

Familiar French Words and Phrases

Bon appétit (bahn a-pay-TEE) Enjoy your meal
Bon mot (bahn MO) Witty remark
Bon voyage (bahn vwa-YAZH) Have a good trip

Carte blanche (kart blansh) Blanket permission

Cause célèbre (koz sə-LEB-rə) Incident or case that arouses public concern

C'est la vie (se lah VEE) That's life

Coup de grace (koo-də-GRAS) Final blow

Crème de la crème (KREM də la KREM) The best of the best

Déjà vu (day-zha VU) Feeling that something has happened before

Enfant terrible (ahn-fahn te-ree-blə) Terrible child, a brat

En masse (ahn MAS) In a group, all together

Esprit de corps (is-PREE də KOR) Good feeling of friendship in a group

Fait accompli (FAYTə-kahm-PLEE) Something already done

Joie de vivre (zhwa də VEEVR) Love of life

Savoir-faire (sa-vwar FAYR) Knows how to act in social settings

Tête à tête (tayt ə TAYT) Head to head meeting

Familiar Latin
Words and Phrases

Ad hoc (ad HAHK) Something for the occasion

Alma mater (al-mə MATər) School one graduates from; also school song. Translated from Latin, alma mater means "soul mother"

Bona fide (BO-nə fīd) Genuine

Curriculum vitae (kə-RIK-yə-ləm VI-tee) A short account of a person's career

De facto (dee FAK-to) In fact, accepted

E pluribus unum (ee PLUR-ə-bəs OO-nəm) One out of many

Ex post facto (eks post FAK-to) After the deed

In loco parentis (in LO-ko pə-RENT-əs) In place of the parents

In toto (in TO-to) Completely

Mea culpa (may-ə KUL-pə) I'm sorry, my fault

Modus operandi (mod-əs ah-pə-RAN-dee) A characteristic method of doing something

Non compos mentis (nahn KAM-pəs MENT-əs) Someone out of his mind or her mind

Persona non grata (pər-SO-nə nahn GRAT-ə) An unwelcome person; one out of favor

Quid pro quo (kwid pro KWO) Something for something

Sine qua non (sin-i kwa NAHN) The essential ingredient

OPENERS AND CLOSERS

The first words of books, poems, and speeches should grab the attention of the reader or listener, and the final words should leave a lasting impression. The closing lines of Martin Luther King's famous "I Have a Dream" speech, for example, are so moving, they have been repeated countless times. Here are some famous openers and closers.

Openers

"In the beginning God created the Heaven and the Earth. . . ."

Opening lines of the Old Testament (Genesis).

"Friends, Romans, countrymen, lend me your ears;
I come to bury Caesar, not to praise him. . . ."

> Opening line of speech given by Mark Antony at the funeral of Julius Caesar in the play *Julius Caesar* by William Shakespeare.

"Call me Ishmael. . . ."

> Opening line of Herman Melville's famous novel, *Moby-Dick*, first published in 1851. (Ishmael is a name meaning outcast or exile.)

"It was the best of times, it was the worst of times, it was the age of wisdom, it was the age of foolishness, it was the epoch of belief, it was the epoch of incredulity, it was the season of Light, it was the season of Darkness, it was the spring of hope, it was the winter of despair. . . ."

> Part of the opening sentence of Charles Dickens's novel *A Tale of Two Cities*, published in 1859.

"Fourscore and seven years ago, our fathers brought forth, upon this continent, a new nation, conceived in Liberty, and dedicated to the proposition that all men are created equal. . . ."

> Opening of President Abraham Lincoln's Gettysburg Address, 1863.

"Give me your tired, your poor,
Your huddled masses yearning to breathe free . . ."

> From Emma Lazarus's poem "The New Colossus," 1884, engraved on the Statue of Liberty.

"That's one small step for a man, one giant leap for mankind."

> The first words of Neil Armstrong when he set foot on the moon, 1969.

"I've never been a quitter . . ."

> Opening line from President Nixon's resignation speech, August 9, 1974.

Closers

"Et tu, Brute?"

> Words uttered by Caesar to Brutus in the play *Julius Caesar* by William Shakespeare. The Latin sentence means "Even you, Brutus?" Caesar was surprised to see Brutus among his assassins.

"I know not what course others may take, but as for me, give me liberty or give me death."

    Closing line of Patrick Henry, American statesman, as he urged the Virginia militia to fight the British, 1775.

"I only regret that I have but one life to lose for my country."

    Last words of Nathan Hale, a colonist who was hanged by the British for being a spy. Revolutionary War, 1776.

"Happy Christmas to all, and to all a good night."

    Last line of poem by Clement C. Moore, "A Visit From St. Nicholas," published in 1823.

". . . that this nation, under God, shall have a new birth of freedom—and that government of the people, by the people, for the people, shall not perish from the earth."

President Abraham Lincoln's closing words in his Gettysburg Address, 1863.

"That was their finest hour."

Closing line of a 1940 speech by British Prime Minister Winston Churchill. He was speaking of British troops in World War II.

"I shall return."

American General Douglas MacArthur's last words after leaving his troops in Corregidor, 1942. (He did return.)

"Free at last, free at last! Thank God Almighty, we are free at last!"

Closing words from Martin Luther King, Jr.'s "I Have a Dream" speech at the 1963 Civil Rights March, Washington, D.C., in which he quotes a spiritual.

THE LANGUAGE OF FOOD

Food is always a popular subject. Here's a chance to get familiar with the language of food. Below you'll discover that the meat of a conch shell becomes scungilli when it's cooked Italian style. And you'll find out what kind of food "Stamp and Go" is and where it originated.

International Snacking Guide

People all over the world eat small foods between or before meals. Here are the names of some traditional snacks from around the world.

Antipasta (Italian)	Italian plates of sliced sausages, pickled onions, beets, peppers and artichokes, cheese, and raw vegetables served with bread.
Dim Sum (Chinese)	This array of hot Chinese snacks combines the sweet with the savory, and includes filled buns, dumplings, and turnovers, which may be baked, steamed, or fried. These morsels are

served with hot tea and enjoyed in the afternoon or as a midnight snack.

High Tea (English)
The English custom of high tea is served in the afternoon and features dainty bite-size "tea" sandwiches and sweet cakes.

Hors d'oeuvres (French)
Appetizers such as bite-size meats, vegetables, and spreads and dips that are served with bread and crackers. Another French appetizer is the canape, which is served in its own bread or pastry.

Meza (Armenian)
Served hot or cold, these Armenian appetizers include foods such as grape leaves stuffed with rice, feta cheese on bread, eggplant, and caviar.

Samosas (Indian)
These are bite-size Indian pastries stuffed with meats and vegetables. They are served with chutney and dipping sauces.

Short Eats (Sri Lanka)	These are tasty snacks served with tea. They're generally served as finger foods and are popular at parties. They include small sandwiches, deviled eggs, meat kebabs, croquettes, and countless others.
Smorgasbord (Swedish)	A spread of open sandwiches, salads, cheeses, pickled fish, and relishes.
Stamp and Go (Jamaican)	A snack of spicy, batter-fried codfish found at bus stops throughout Jamaica. Jamaicans are known to jump off the bus to get a "Stamp and Go" and then get back aboard to continue their journey.
Tapas (Spanish)	Spanish tapas bars serve snacks before lunch and dinner. The small appetizers include grilled mushrooms, spicy snails, and garlic shrimp.
Zensai (Japanese)	Japanese tidbits of vinegared rice topped with raw seafood and vegetables that are served as snacks at a sushi bar.

Dictionary of Uncommon Fruits and Vegetables

There's a vast market of fruits and vegetables available in America that aren't commonly grown here. Here's a list of some of these exotic fruits and vegetables that can be eaten out of hand, tossed into salads, or served with dip.

Vegetables

Arugula. A mustard-flavored green that originated in the Mediterranean area. Its bitter flavor adds zest to a salad.

Bok Choy. Smooth white stalks with soft, pale green leaves. This Chinese favorite is crunchy, mild, and juicy.

Daikon Radish. Shaped like a carrot but white in color, this Oriental radish can be eaten in salads or on a raw vegetable platter. It's low in calories and high in vitamin C. Its taste is mild, juicy, and crisp.

Fennel. Native to Italy, this celerylike vegetable is distinguished by a green feathery top. The taste is licoricelike, and the texture is crunchy.

Hearts of Palm. These are the ivory-colored interiors of palm trees with a flavor somewhat like an artichoke. Usually purchased in a can.

Jicama (HEE-kə-mə). A crunchy, juicy, somewhat sweet root from Mexico that's perfect with dips.

Kohlrabi (KOL-ra-bee). Crisp, light, and crunchy. This round root from Asia has a radish flavor. Most are light green in color; some are purple.

Radicchio (ra-DEE-kee-o). A red-leafed chicory from Italy which adds a bittersweet flavor to a salad bowl.

Swiss Chard. A large-leafed stalk from the beet family, chard is green with red streaks. Raw Swiss chard has a beetlike flavor and a spinachlike texture. It adds zest to salads and may also be added to soups or sautéed.

Fruits

Carambola (Kar-əm-BOL-ə) (Star Fruit). A yellow, five-ribbed fruit with a floral aroma popular in Asia, South America, and the Caribbean.

Cherimoya (cher-ə-MOY-ə). Also known as a custard apple because of the texture of its cream-colored flesh. The exterior is tough and green. It may be eaten with a spoon to work around the shiny black seeds. The flavor is sweet and tropical.

Clementine. A tangerine that is seedless, easily peeled, and tasty. Clementines originated in Tangiers.

Kiwi (KEE-we). This tasty, sweet egg-shaped fruit has a fuzzy brown exterior that conceals green flesh studded with black, edible seeds. It is native to New Zealand, where it is known as a Chinese gooseberry.

Kumquat. This golden-orange, small round fruit is from Japan. It may be eaten whole just as a grape is eaten.

Mango. A tropical fruit native to Southeast Asia with a yellow-orange skin, and yellow flesh surrounding a large flat narrow pit. The fruit is fragrant and juicy and sweet.

Papaya. A tropical fruit grown in Hawaii that is very digestible. When ripe the skin is yellow-green. The center cavity is made up of black-gray seeds.

Passion Fruit. The wrinkled, purple-brown exterior of this tropical fruit surrounds a yellowish interior with edible seeds. The flavor is both acidic and sweet.

Ugli. This hybrid of a grapefruit and tangerine comes from Jamaica. It is called ugly because of its bumpy, greenish yellow skin. It is the size of a grapefruit, or large orange, and has a pleasant citrus flavor.

Familiar Foods with Unknown Ingredients

Here is a list of foods that you may have tasted without knowing exactly what's in them.

Bouillabaisse A Mediterranean fish soup made of a variety of fish, flavored with tomatoes, garlic, and onions.

Calamari The term for squid used by people in Mediterranean countries. It is often served fried with sauce on pasta, or boiled and cold in seafood salads.

Caviar

Salted fish roe (eggs) from large fish such as sturgeon, salmon, and whitefish. Black caviar is from sturgeon; orange caviar from salmon; and golden caviar from whitefish.

Chitterlings (Chitlins)

The small intestines of a pig. Chitterlings are popular in the South, where they are deep fried and simmered in sauce.

Chutney

A chunky relish made of fruits, vegetables, sugar, vinegar, and spices. Chutneys are served as accompaniments to meat and poultry.

Conch (Kank)

The meat of a large spiral-shelled mollusk. The Italians call it scungilli and cook it in tomato sauce.

Finnan Haddie

Smoked haddock, a fish dish named for the fish and the seaport town Findon, Scotland, where it originated.

Foie Gras (fwa GRA)

This French delicacy is the enlarged liver of a goose. The liver is enlarged by force-feeding.

Gnocchi (NYO-kee)

This Italian potato dumpling is popular in regions of Italy, where it is served with a sauce.

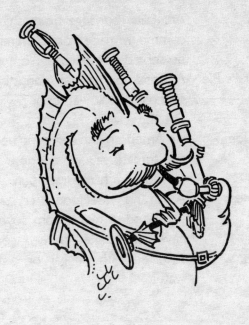

Hominy

The whole kernels of dried corn with germs and hulls removed. Ground hominy is known as grits.

Hummus (HOO-məs)

Creamy sauce made of chick-peas flavored with lemon juice, garlic, and olive oil. When sesame seed paste is added to this sauce, it becomes tahini (*hummus bi tahini*).

Kippers

This is smoked herring, a traditional British breakfast food. The herring is split open and fried in butter.

Lox

Salmon that is smoked and soaked in brine. "Belly lox" is the term for the cut of the underpart of the salmon.

Polenta	An Italian porridge or mush. It is most commonly made from cornmeal and can be served hot or cold.
Shepherd's Pie	A British baked dish consisting of seasoned ground meat topped with mashed potatoes.
Sloppy Joe	An American dish of ground beef, onions, and tomato sauce made in a skillet and served on a hamburger bun.
Sweetmeat	A rich and sweet food or crystalized fruit.
Tofu	This food is made from soybeans that have been soaked, pureed, cooked, and solidified with vinegar or distilled seawater.

Diner Lingo

When you're eating in a coffee shop or diner, you may hear the staff calling out orders in an unfamiliar language. Here is some of the lingo used in diners.

"Adam and Eve on a raft"	Poached eggs on an English muffin
"All the way"	A sandwich made with lettuce, tomato, onion, and mayonnaise
"Apple grease"	Butter

"Bowl of red"	Chili
"British"	English muffin
"Bun pup"	Hot dog
"Burn"	Toast it
"China"	Rice pudding
"City juice"	Water
"Clean up the kitchen"	Hash
"Crowd"	Three of anything
"Dog biscuit"	Cracker
"Down"	Toasted
"Drag it through the garden"	Add lettuce, tomatoes, and onions to a sandwich
"Draw one"	Coffee

"Eighty-one"	Glass of water
"Eighty-six"	The kitchen is out of the order or cancel
"High and dry"	Toasted bread, no butter
"Hold the nail"	No ice
"In the alley"	Served as a side dish
"Irish turkey"	Corn beef and cabbage
"Lox box"	Lox and cream cheese on a bagel
"Mike and Ike"	Salt and pepper
"Pistol"	Pastrami on rye bread
"Radio"	Tuna on rye
"Sinkers and suds"	Doughnuts and coffee
"Squeeze one"	Orange juice
"Stiff"	Customer who doesn't tip
"Thirty-one"	Three eggs on one plate
"Tubers and repeaters"	Franks and beans
"Whiskey down"	Rye toast

Misnamed Foods

These are common foods whose names don't quite match what you find inside.

Boston Cream Pie. Boston cream pie is a cake, not a pie. It is made of two layers of white cake with a vanilla cream filling and a chocolate icing.

Buttermilk. There is no butter in buttermilk. Originally buttermilk was the name of the liquid by-product that came from making butter. Today skim milk is treated with a bacteria to produce this thick, faintly sour-tasting drink that is low in fat and nutritious.

English Muffin. What Americans call an English muffin, the English call a crumpet. In both England and the U.S., a muffin is a quick bread, containing no yeast, baked in a muffin tin.

Headcheese. Not a cheese but sausage made from calf's or pig's head and other parts, then molded together with a jellied broth.

Lemon Sole. The lemon in lemon sole comes from the French word *limande*, which means any kind of flat fish. There is no lemon in lemon sole.

Plum Pudding. A Christmas pudding containing no

plums. It is made with candied fruits, raisins, nuts, and spices.

Refried Beans. A Mexican dish of mashed and fried beans. The beans are not fried twice. The term is a mistranslation for the Spanish *frijoles refritos*, which means "well-fried beans." The term was first printed in 1957.

Sweetbreads. A sweetbread is the pancreas of a young animal, usually a calf. It is not a bread and it is not sweet; it is served as a meat.

Tangelo. A tangelo is a hybrid of an orange and a grape-fruit. There is no flavor of tangerine in this fruit.

Tigers Milk. Tigers Milk has nothing to do with a tiger and very little to do with milk. This flavored energy drink or bar is made of soybean concentrate and may contain some dried skim milk.

Wild Rice. Wild rice is not a rice. It is a wild grass that grows in water, mostly in Minnesota and Canada.

Five Cuisines of the World

(What you will eat if you eat out)

Chinese Cuisine

The culinary art of China is meant to satisfy five senses. Its preparation involves the sound of sizzling food, the sight of many colored foods artfully arranged, the smell of sea-sonings, the taste of contrasting flavors such as sweet and sour, and the use of foods with varied textures and shapes. Food is traditionally cooked quickly because of a once lim-ited supply of cooking fuel. All Chinese food combines balance, proportion, and harmony. Because of the great size of China, there are several different types of cuisine, each distinctive to its region. These different cuisines are as follows:

Canton. This regional food was the first to be introduced to America, which is why it is the most familiar to Americans. Cantonese food is marked by light flavors and delicate sauces. Canton, in southwest China, is a seacoast region, thus Cantonese cooking emphasizes seafoods flavored with soy sauce, oyster sauce, or fermented black beans. A classic Cantonese dish is subgum (stir-fried noodles topped with meat).

Mandarin and Peking. These are northern regions where wheat, rather than rice, is the staple. Pancakes, noodles, and dumplings originated here. Dishes are not as frequently stir-fried. They are flavored with garlic, ginger, onions, and wine. Lamb and duck are popular meats in these regions.

Shanghai. The eastern region of Shanghai is rich in seafood, agriculture, and produce. Ginger, garlic, and green onions are the main seasonings. Typical foods of Shanghai are spring rolls (egg rolls), wonton, and sweet and sour fish.

Szechuan and Hunan. These south central inland regions are characterized by hot, spicy, strongly flavored foods. Chili peppers, hot pepper, and sesame oil are used to produce pungent tart and sweet flavors. Typical dishes are hot and sour soup, chicken with hot peppers, and crispy spicy fish.

Indian Cuisine

The food of India is distinguished by region as well as religion. Muslims are forbidden to eat pork but eat beef and other meats. Hindus eat no beef because they consider cows to be sacred animals. Some Buddhists are strict vegetarians who avoid all animal products, including eggs and milk.

In northern India yogurt and *ghee* (clarified butter) are used in dishes and *chapati* (bread) is more widely eaten than

rice. In southern India coconut plays an important role and rice is the basis of the meal.

The outstanding feature of all Indian cooking is the use of spices such as mustard seeds, coriander, cumin, and hot chilis. Also, rice or bread is the main part of the meal. The curries, meat, fish, or vegetables are served in small portions.

In India food is eaten with fingers—those of the right hand only. Often banana leaves or breads serve as plates or scoops.

Italian Cuisine

There is no such thing as Italian cooking. The cooking of Italy varies by region and city; each has a distinct approach to food. Although the cities of Naples and Venice both

specialize in seafoods, the ways they are prepared are completely different. In the northern dairy land, butter is the fat used for cooking, and *risotto* (a rice dish) and *polenta* (corn mush) are the staples. In the central and southern regions, olives provide oil for cooking and *macaroni* (pasta) is the staple. In Naples tomatoes are used in almost every dish.

An Italian meal involves many courses of food. The first is either a pasta or a soup. The second is often a meat or fish accompanied by two vegetables as side dishes. Salad and dessert follow.

Japanese Cuisine

The simplicity of Japanese food distinguishes it from all other Asian foods. Traditional Japanese cooking is done over or in water rather than oil. Seaweed is used to flavor dishes or eaten on its own. *Tofu* is a mainstay of the diet and is served morning, noon, and night. *Miso* (bean paste) and *shoyu* (soy sauce) from the soybean used for tofu are also fundamental to Japanese food. When Japanese foods are fried as in tempura, they are light and crisp. Distinctive Japanese foods are: *sashimi*, which is raw fish; *sushi*, vinegared rice patties topped with raw vegetables or seafood; *yakitori*, foods marinated, fried, and glazed with a special soy sauce.

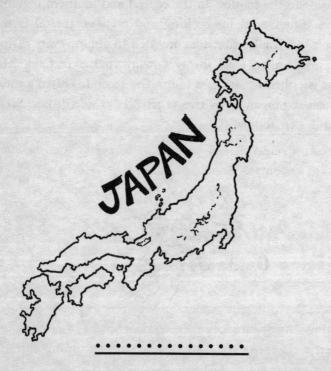

Mexican Cuisine

Over one hundred kinds of chilies are found in Mexico. It is no wonder that chilies are the dominant seasoning in Mexican cuisine. *Mole poblano* is the national dish of Mexico. It is a chicken dish cooked in a dark sauce of chili, chocolate, and spices. The *tortilla*, a thin pancake made of ground corn or wheat, serves as the basis for many Mexican dishes: *tostadas* are crisply fried tortillas with garnishes; *tacos* are tortillas wrapped around a filling; *enchilladas* are tortillas dipped in chili sauce and filled with cheese or meat.

Other common Mexican foods are *burritos*, which are tacos made with wheat tortillas; *chorizo*, a spicy pork sausage; and *tamales*, the fiesta food. *Tamales* are made from wheat or corn dough, chilies, and meat. They are then steamed inside a cornhusk or banana leaf.

Dining Alfresco (Eating Outdoors)

There are different names for different styles of outdoor eating. Americans consider outdoor eating a celebration. Here are some of the distinctive names for dining alfresco.

Clambake. The early American settlers learned this method of cooking from the native tribes of the eastern seaboard. Today's popular New England clambake is derived from the Indians' tradition of digging pits, laying seaweed over hot stones, and steaming corn and shellfish in these pits.

Barbecue. This all-American pastime originated with Native Americans and was named by the Spanish. When the Spanish explorers saw the American Indians grilling or smoking meat and fish outdoors, they called it *"barbacoa."*

Luau. This is a Hawaiian or Polynesian feast. Guests sit on the ground and eat and drink to the accompaniment of music and dancing.

Picnic. Originally, a picnic meant each guest brought a different dish to dinner. In England, by the late eighteenth century, it was a gathering of refined people to eat elaborate cold dishes outside. Today a picnic is an outing or excursion with food eaten outdoors.

Tailgate. This is an eating party held in the parking lot of a stadium before a sports event. The food may be cold or cooked on a portable grill. The back or tailgate of a station wagon is lowered for sitting or serving, thus the name tailgate.

Foods on the Tongue

These are expressions that refer to food but don't necessarily have anything to do with cooking or eating.

Food Phrase	Meaning
Apple of one's eye	someone who is adored
Apple pie order	exact, orderly arrangement
Bring home the bacon	make money
Cook one's goose	destroy one's future expectations or good name
Cook up	create

Cool as a cucumber	very calm
Cornball	corny, trite
Eating high off the hog	living well
Egg on	urge
Full of baloney	worthless; not reliable as a source of truth or information
Full of beans	full of pep
Full of prunes	being foolish
Half-baked	not thought out
Ham it up	exaggerate
Hot dog!	hurrah
Hot potato	a question that causes a dispute and is dangerous to deal with
Lemon	something that turns out badly
Meat and potatoes	the basics
Polish the apple	to try to win favors by flattery
Rotten egg	a bad person
Salad days	young and green; inexperienced
Souped up	more powerful
Talk turkey	talk in a businesslike way
Take with a grain of salt	believe only in part

SIGNIFICANT NUMBERS
••••••••••••••••••••••••••••••••••••

Sometimes certain numbers bring to mind a phrase from a rhyme, or a character in a story. Numbers can even help us to remember how many seas there are, or how many questions a reporter should ask.

007. This is the secret agent number of James Bond. He is a famous character in Ian Fleming's novels. The numbers 00 signify that he is an agent who is licensed to kill.

3. In the nursery rhyme *"Three Men in a Tub,"* there are three men: the butcher, the baker, and the candlestick maker.

In the story of *"The Three Little Pigs,"* one pig builds a house of straw, one a house of sticks, and one a house of brick.

In the children's song *"Three Blind Mice,"* the three mice run after the farmer's wife, who cuts off their tails with a carving knife.

In the story of "Goldilocks," she visits the home of the *three bears*. They are the papa, the mama, and the baby bear.

The Three Musketeers, from the novel by Alexandre Dumas, are Athos, Aramis, and Porthos.

3-D signifies the three dimensions of an object. They are height, width, and length.

The *three R's* of learning are reading, 'riting, and 'rithmetic.

The *Three Stooges* of comedy fame are Moe, Curly, and Larry.

The *Three Wise Men* who traveled to the stable to see Jesus Christ at his birth were Casper, Melchior, and Balthasar. The *three gifts* they brought were gold, frankincense, and myrrh.

The *Three Wise Monkeys* are Mizaru ("see no evil"), Mikazaru ("hear no evil"); and Mazaru ("speak no evil").

4. The *Four Evangelists*, the authors of the gospels of the New Testament of the Bible, were Matthew, Mark, Luke, and John.

The *Four Horsemen* are symbolic figures in the Bible. They represent the evils to come at the end of the world. The rider on the black horse represents famine, the rider on the pale horse represents death, the rider on the red horse represents war, and the rider on the white horse represents conquest.

The *Four Freedoms* listed in U.S. President Franklin D. Roosevelt's 1941 speech are: Freedom of speech and expression; Freedom of religion; Freedom from want; and Freedom from fear.

5. The first *Five Books of the Old Testament*, also known as the Pentateuch, are: Genesis, Exodus, Leviticus, Numbers, and Deuteronomy.

The *Five Nations* that made up the Iroquois league of Native Americans were: Seneca, Mohawk, Oneida, Onondaga, and Cayuga.

The *Five Little Peppers* in the stories by Margaret Sydney were: Polly, Ben, Phronsie, Joel, and Davie.

6. The *Six Questions* a reporter asks are: who, what, when, where, why, and how.

7. The *Seven Deadly Sins* are: pride, avarice, sloth, envy, gluttony, lust, and wrath.

The *Seven Dwarfs* in the Walt Disney version of *Snow White* are: Bashful, Doc, Dopey, Grumpy, Happy, Sleepy, and Sneezy.

The *Seven Continents* are: Asia, Africa, Antarctica, Australia, Europe, North America, and South America.

The *Seven Seas* are: Antarctic, Arctic, North Atlantic, South Atlantic, Indian, North Pacific, and South Pacific.

The *Seven Wonders* of the Ancient World were: the Pyramids, the Hanging Gardens of Babylon, Statue of Zeus, Temple of Diana at Ephesus, Mausoleum at Halicarnassus, Colossus at Rhodes, and Lighthouse at Pharos.

The *Seven Works of Mercy* are: bury the dead, clothe the naked, feed the hungry, give drink to the thirsty, house the homeless, tend the sick, visit the afflicted.

7x is the secret ingredient in Coca-Cola.

10. The *Ten Plagues of Egypt* were: water becomes blood, frogs, lice, cattle murrain, flies swarm, sores and boils, hail and fire, locusts, darkness, slaying of the firstborn.

12. The *Twelve Apostles of Jesus Christ* were: Peter, James, John, Andrew, Philip, Bartholomew, Matthew, James, Thomas, Simon, Judas Iscariot, and Thaddeus.

The *"Twelve Days of Christmas"* is a carol that lists these twelve gifts: one partridge, two turtledoves, three French hens, four calling birds, five golden rings, six geese a-laying, seven swans a-swimming, eight maids a-milking, nine ladies dancing, ten lords a-leaping, eleven pipers piping, twelve drummers drumming.

13. A baker's dozen is *thirteen*, rather than twelve.

15. *"Fifteen Men* on a dead man's chest/Yo, ho, ho and a bottle of rum" are words from the pirates' song in the novel *Treasure Island*, by Robert Louis Stevenson.

22. *Catch-22* is a war novel by Joseph Heller. A "catch-22" is a ridiculous situation that puts a person in a double bind; for example, one can't get a job without experience, yet one can't get experience without a job.

30. For *thirty pieces of silver*, Judas Iscariot betrayed Jesus Christ.

40. In the biblical story of Noah and his Ark, it rained for *forty days and forty nights*.

After Jesus was baptized by John the Baptist, he went alone into the desert for *forty* days.

The children of Israel spent *forty* years in the wilderness. These lines are from the song about Lizzie Borden, who was accused of killing her parents with an ax:

"Lizzie Borden took an ax,
And gave her mother *forty whacks*;
And when she saw what she had done,
She gave her father forty-one."

76. *"Seventy-six trombones* led the big parade." These are the lyrics of a song from the musical *The Music Man*, by Meredith Wilson.

88. The number of keys on a piano. *"Eighty-eight"* is slang for piano.

89. U.S. homesteaders who settled in Oklahoma in 1889 were called *eighty-niners*.

WORD PEOPLE (NAMES THAT BECAME WORDS)

The names of some people from history and literature have come to represent a certain type of personality, or to mean a certain person or thing. Below you can find out why a John Hancock is a signature, why we call a handsome man an Adonis, and why a woman who isn't exactly royalty is sometimes called a Queen of Sheba.

Real Word People

Caesar (SEE-zer). Julius Caesar was the first of the Roman emperors. The eleven rulers of Rome who followed him were also called Caesar. A "caesar" is a powerful ruler or dictator.

Casanova. Giovanni Casanova de Seingalt was an eighteenth-century Italian. He was an amorous adventurer who wrote a memoir of his life and loves. A "casanova" is a male lover, usually an unprincipled one.

Cicero (SIS-ə-ro). Marcus Tullius Cicero was a Roman statesman and orator who lived in the century before Christ. He made many inspiring speeches to the Roman Senate. "Ciceronian" refers to a speech that is clear and powerful.

Einstein. Albert Einstein was an American citizen who was born in Germany in 1879. His theories of space and time were major scientific breakthroughs. He is considered one of the greatest minds of all time. An "Einstein" is someone who is a genius.

Epicure (EP-i-kyur). Epicurus was a Greek philosopher who lived from 341 to 270 B.C. His philosophy embraced the idea of making life happy and pleasurable. An "epicure" is a person with refined tastes, especially in food and drink.

Geronimo. Geronimo was an Apache chief who lived in the late 1800s. He was one of the last great warriors in Native Americans' fight for their land. "Geronimo" is a battle cry.

John Hancock. John Hancock lived in eighteenth-century America. He was a politician and leader of the Continental Congress, and the first to sign the Declaration of Inde-

pendence. His signature was very bold and large. A "John Hancock" is a signature.

Machiavelli (Mahk-ee-ə-VEL-ee).

Niccolò Machiavelli was a politician and philosopher who lived in Italy from 1469 to 1527. His most famous book, *The Prince*, described how to gain and keep power through cunning and deceit. "Machiavellian" describes an amoral person or deed.

Napoleon.

Napoleon Bonaparte was a French general and emperor in the early 1800s. His rise to power was swift, and as emperor, he conquered much of Europe. "Napoleonic" refers to delusions of grandeur. Napoleon was short in stature. Overly aggressive short men are said to have a "Napoleon complex."

Queen of Sheba.

The Queen of Sheba lived in the tenth century B.C. in the Middle East. She was famous for her beauty and splendor. A female who acts like royalty is referred to as the "Queen of Sheba."

Fictional Word People

Achilles (ə-KIL-eez).

Achilles was a warrior in Greek mythology. When he was a baby his mother held him by

his heel and washed him in the river Styx to make him invulnerable. Only his heel remained vulnerable. An "Achilles heel" is a weak point in a person's character.

Adonis. In Greek mythology, Adonis was a boy of exceptional beauty. An "Adonis" is a remarkably handsome man.

Atlas. In Greek mythology, Atlas held the earth and sky up on his shoulders. He was often pictured on early maps. An atlas is a book of maps.

Cassandra. In Greek mythology, Cassandra was a Trojan princess who had the power of prophecy. She predicted the fall of Troy. A "Cassandra" is one who predicts bad news.

Cinderella. A fairy tale tells of a young girl, Cinderella, who is mistreated and made to work very hard in her stepmother's house. With the help of her fairy godmother, Cinderella meets a prince who marries her and takes her away from misery. A "Cinderella" is one who undergoes great changes and achieves recognition and happiness.

Frankenstein. In *Frankenstein*, a novel by Mary Wollstonecraft Shelley, the main character, Dr. Frankenstein, creates a manlike monster and brings it to life. Although Frankenstein is the doctor and not the monster in the book, people commonly call a monster-man, a "Frankenstein."

Gargantua (gar-GANCH-wə). Gargantua is a character in a fifteenth-century comic novel of the same name written by François Rabelais. Gargantua was a king who was mammoth in size and appetite. "Gargantuan" refers to anything huge.

Hercules (HER-kyə-leez). In Greek mythology, Hercules was known for his great strength and bravery. As a baby in a cradle he strangled serpents. As an adult he performed twelve mighty labors. "Herculean" refers to things of great power or difficulty.

Jekyll and Hyde. In his nineteenth-century novel *The Strange Case of Dr. Jekyll and Mr. Hyde*, Robert Louis Stevenson tells the story of one man with a split personality, part good, part evil. A "Jekyll and Hyde" is a person with two extremely different natures.

Midas. Midas was a greedy king from Greek mythology. He was granted a wish so that everything he touched turned to gold. A person who gets riches easily is said to have the "Midas touch."

Peeping Tom. In the old English legend, Lady Godiva rode naked through the streets with only her long hair to cover her. Tom, the town tailor, was the only one who dared to peek at her. A "Peeping Tom" is one who peeks at things or people that are private.

Pollyanna. Pollyanna is the title character in the children's book by Eleanor Porter. Pollyanna, an orphan, is always cheerful despite her difficult life. A "Pollyanna" is a person who is blindly optimistic.

Scrooge. Ebenezer Scrooge is a mean-spirited, miserly person in *A Christmas Carol*, a story by Charles Dickens. A "scrooge" is a miser.

Biblical Word People

Job. In the Old Testament of the Bible, Job, a happy and prosperous man, is severely tested by the Devil. Even in his most desperate moments, Job will not curse God. A long-suffering person is called a "Job."

Methuselah (me-THOO-zə-lə). According to the Bible, Methuselah, descendant of Seth, lived 969 years. "As old as Methuselah" refers to very old age.

Solomon. The Old Testament tells of Solomon, a wise king. When two women claimed to be the mother of the same baby, he was asked to decide which was the real one. Solomon offered to cut the baby in half and give half to each woman. The wisdom of his suggestion is apparent when the real mother offered to give up the baby rather than see it killed. A wise person is said to have "the wisdom of Solomon."

MNEMONICS

••

Mnemonics (ni-MON-iks) are memory devices that you can use to help you remember some people, places, and things. With some of the rhymes, sentences, and words below, you can memorize dates and facts.

1. *All the letters of the alphabet in one sentence*
   The quick brown fox jumps over a lazy dog.

2. *Colors of the spectrum*
   Red, Orange, Yellow, Green, Blue, Indigo, Violet.
   Richard of York Gains Battle in Vain.

3. *Directions listed on a compass in clockwise order*
   North, East, South, West
   Never Eat Shredded Wheat.

4. *Four Major Vocal Parts*
   Soprano, Tenor, Alto, Bass
   S T A B

5. *Great Lakes*
   Huron, Ontario, Michigan, Erie, Superior
   H O M E S

6. *How to set the clocks to adjust daylight saving time*
    Spring ahead; fall back.

7. *Number of days in the months of the year*
    Thirty days hath September,
    April, June, and November,
    All the rest have thirty-one,
    Excepting February alone.

8. *The order of the planets from the sun*
    Mercury, Venus, Earth, Mars, Jupiter,
    Saturn, Uranus, Neptune, Pluto
    *My Very Educated Mother Just Showed
    Us Nine Planets.*

9. *Original Thirteen States in the order in
    which they joined the Union*

Del., Penn., N.J.
  Led the way.
George, Conn., Mass.
  Next in class.
Seven, Mary
  Eight, South Carrie.
New Hamp., nine on
  The founding slate.
Virginia ten.
  New York was late.
N.C., R.I.
  They cast the die
And saved the day
  For the U.S.A.

10.   *The spelling rule for using I and E in the
same word*
I before E,
Except after C,
And when pronounced A,
As in neighbor and weigh.

11.   *Year Columbus sailed to America*
In fourteen hundred and ninety-two
Columbus sailed the ocean blue.

12.   *Year American Civil War ended*
When the Union did survive
'Twas eighteen hundred sixty-five.

13.   *Year of the great fire of London*
In sixteen hundred sixty-six, London
burned like rotten sticks

INDEX
• •

ABOUT THE AUTHORS

MARGO MCLOONE BASTA has coauthored many nonfiction books for children. She is a former New York City junior high school teacher who now lives and writes in Woodstock, New York, with her husband and three children.

ALICE SIEGEL is the coauthor of many nonfiction books for children. She is a reading specialist in the Greenwich, Connecticut, public schools and has devoted the past twenty years to writing children's reference books. These books answer the questions children most frequently ask. Her hope is that they will empower children to seek and find their own answers.

She lives in Scarsdale with her husband and three sons.